D063641?

Columbia University

Contributions to Education

Teachers College Series

No. 213

AMS PRESS

NEW YORK

THE WORK
OF
BOARDS OF EDUCATION

BY

HANS C. OLSEN, Ph.D.

DIRECTOR OF TEACHER TRAINING
STATE TEACHERS COLLEGE, KEARNEY, NEBRASKA

Teachers College, Columbia University
Contributions to Education, No. 213

Bureau of Publications
Teachers College, Columbia University
NEW YORK CITY
1926

Library of Congress Cataloging in Publication Data

Olsen, Hans Christian, 1892–
    The work of boards of education.

    Reprint of the 1926 ed., issued in series: Teachers
College, Columbia University. Contributions to
education, no. 213.
    Originally presented as the author's thesis,
Columbia.
    Bibliography: p.
    1. School boards. 2. School management and
organization--United States. I. Title. II. Series:
Columbia University. Teachers College. Contributions
to education, no. 213.
LB2831.O44 1972   379'.1531   77-177134

ISBN 0-404-55213-7

Reprinted by Special Arrangement with Teachers
College Press, New York, New York

From the edition of 1926, New York
First AMS edition published in 1972
Manufactured in the United States

AMS PRESS, INC.
NEW YORK, N. Y.   10003

ACKNOWLEDGMENTS

The author desires to acknowledge his indebtedness to Professor George D. Strayer for first suggesting the problem and for his constant assistance and encouragement during the prosecution of the study.

He is grateful to Professor N. L. Engelhardt for his unfailing aid in securing needed data and for his constructive criticisms at all times.

To Professors Edward S. Evenden, David Snedden, J. R. McGaughy, Carter Alexander, and Paul Mort, he wishes to acknowledge the useful and stimulating suggestions they have so generously contributed.

H. C. O.

CONTENTS

Contents

THE WORK OF BOARDS OF EDUCATION

CHAPTER I

INTRODUCTION

It is now fully recognized that a board of education cannot itself properly manage the schools under its control. A professionally trained chief executive officer is therefore employed to administer the schools under the direction of the board of education. But the proper relationship between a school board and its superintendent of schools has never been adequately determined.

The following sample extracts from current literature on educational administration present evidence as to the need for specific and right allocation of duties and responsibilities to the board of education and to its superintendent of schools:

I appreciate, however, that probably a misconception of what things are within the province of the superintendent, and what within the province of the board is where we sometimes come to grief.[1]

I am convinced that another long step in advance may now be taken if school boards and superintendents will sit down together . . . for the purpose of facing squarely and frankly the problem of administration itself in relation to our schools and in an effort to discover ways of improving present practice and of setting in motion a program of control and administrative procedures that will make a permanent contribution to the stability of the schools and the efficiency of their management. *This will entail a critical and impersonal analysis of the situation as it exists, the results desired, the work to be done, the relationship of responsibilities, the degree to which it is understood that these responsibilities are delegated, and the adequacy of the present organization policies in general.*[2]

The right relationship between boards of education and superintendents of schools will come to exist when boards of education cease to think of their function as having to do with the execution of the policies they adopt; when they scrutinize carefully each proposal brought to them by the superintendent of schools, and having passed upon it stand fast. . . .[3]

[1] Jesse Earle (Member, Board of Education, Janesville, Wisconsin). "What About School Boards and Superintendents?" *American School Board Journal*, 68: 42, July, 1924.
[2] J. W. Studebaker (Superintendent of Schools, Des Moines, Iowa). "School Board Organization and the Superintendent." (Address delivered before The Department of Superintendence of The National Education Association at Chicago in 1924 and published in *American School Board Journal*, 68: 37, April, 1924.)
[3] George D. Strayer. "The Relation of Administrative Officers to Boards of Education." N. E. A. Department of Superintendence *First Yearbook*, 1: 162, 1923.

1

It is quite obvious that in the development of a plan for securing the best educational results for the State, no plan can be tolerated which will not definitely place the responsibility for school efficiency upon the superintendent and the board of education. *Part of the problem which presents itself . . . has to do with the specific division of these powers between these two outstanding centers of responsibility.*[4]

Much remains to be done in defining clearly the relationship which should exist between boards of education and their chief executive officer. It would be well if this definition were made so clear and so commonly accepted by members of the profession that no competent man would be willing to accept the position of superintendent of schools without having it understood that the board of education accepted the relationship as defined by the profession. The effect would be most salutary. It is unfortunate that as the situation is at present a board that usurps the function of the executive, and on that account forces him out of his position, may confidently expect to find that other competent men are willing and anxious to accept the position so vacated.[5]

If administrative authority is divided . . . in the relation of the board to the superintendent . . . ineffectiveness, misunderstanding, friction, and controversy will be the inevitable results.[6]

How the problem of proper relationship between a board of education and its superintendent of schools has developed can be understood from a brief analysis of some of the important studies that have been made in the field of educational administration.

In 1923 Dr. Bennett C. Douglass in his study on "The Status of the Superintendent"[7] wrote as follows of Arthur H. Chamberlain's historical study entitled *The Growth of Responsibility and Enlargement of Power of the City School Superintendent*[8]

Mr. Chamberlain traced the origin of the superintendent's power. He found that the history of city school superintendency began in 1837. He presents evidence to indicate that education is a function of the state. *He argues that the superintendent from the first has been a leader educationally, that a proper relation must be established between the superintendent and the school board, and responsibility must be definitely fixed.* In the chapter on conclusions the council form of organization composed of supervisors and representatives of elementary and secondary teachers is outlined.

[4] Charles E. Chadsey. "The Report of the Committee on the Status of the Superintendent." N. E. A. Department of Superintendence *First Yearbook*, 1: 156, 1923.
[5] George D. Strayer. "The Relation of Administrative Officers to Boards of Education." N. E. A. Department of Superintendence *First Yearbook*, 1: 160, 1923.
[6] Fred M. Hunter (Superintendent of Schools, Oakland, California). "Professional Leadership of Superintendent." *American Educational Digest*, 44: 292, March, 1925.
[7] Bennett C. Douglass. "The Status of the Superintendent." N. E. A. Department of Superintendence *First Yearbook*, 1: 4–152, 1923.
[8] Arthur H. Chamberlain. *The Growth of Responsibility and Enlargement of Power of the City School Superintendent.* University of California Press, Berkeley, Calif., 1913.

In 1917 Dr. William W. Theisen in his study entitled *The City Superintendent and the Board of Education* arrived at the following conclusions and recommendations:

1. That a board of education should endeavor to discover its own proper duties and those that should be delegated to professional executive officers.
2. That its own function is first of all
   a. to choose a professionally trained chief executive, centralize authority and responsibility for results in him, and expect him to initiate all policies; and then
   b. to debate such proposed policies with him in the light of definite objective evidence and to provide the legislation necessary to secure efficient results.
3. That a board of education need wait for no precedent to adopt a form of administrative organization in which the professional superintendent is made the administrative leader and chief executive of the system, and in which the board itself serves in an advisory and legislative capacity and acts only through its chief executive. Such precedent is amply provided by successful business organizations.[9]

Dr. John Cayce Morrison in 1922 summarized the results of his study entitled *The Legal Status of the Superintendent of Schools* as follows:

a. Responsibility for local administration of schools was first vested in municipal or civil officers who had been chosen primarily for the performance of other duties.
b. Gradually, as schools developed, responsibility for direction and supervision of instructional activities was vested in officials whose sole public responsibility was limited to the schools.
c. These lay boards were given power to delegate their responsibility to small committees or to a committee of one.
d. This one official developed into the professionally trained executive known in every state as the city school superintendent.
e. As society adds more and more responsibility to the public school system, the need of better trained and more responsible administrative leadership of schools is recognized.
f. This responsible leadership should extend to all phases of school activity. All dual responsibility should be eliminated.
g. The laws governing school administration should be formulated to build up this responsible leadership and to safeguard the public interest.[10]

In his study on *The Status of the Superintendent*, Dr. Bennett C. Douglass summarizes as follows his findings and conclusions

---

[9] William W. Theisen. *The City Superintendent and the Board of Education.* Teachers College, Columbia University, 1917.
[10] John Cayce Morrison. *The Legal Status of the City Superintendent of Schools.* Teachers College, Columbia University, 1922.

that bear on the relationship between a board of education and its superintendent of schools:

The ten functions of school administration in which superintendents report that they most frequently exercise authority to initiate, execute, or approve show the degree in which superintendents exercise leadership and the technical character of their work.

The fact that the nature of the superintendent's work is essentially that of leadership is further emphasized by the fact that the part performed is chiefly that of initiative.

The source from which the superintendent's authority is derived is much more largely from common consent than from state law or resolution of the board of education.

The superintendent should be regarded not only as professional leader of the supervisory and instructional staff, but as the executive officer of the board of education in advancing the educational interests of the community.

Most favorable conditions for performing the superintendent's work: (a) All the educational activities of the city should be centered in the office of the superintendent of schools; (b) The administrative work of the superintendent should be based upon principles of business administration. Certain authorities should be delegated to competent subordinates; (c) The superintendent should have power to initiate and execute the appointments of assistant superintendents, business managers, principals, teachers, and all other employees whose work is vital in the development of an educational program. He should also have the privilege of recommendations for transfer and dismissal of these educational workers: (d) The budget should be prepared under the direction of the superintendent for presentation to the board of education. (e) The superintendent should have power to initiate new policies and to make rules and regulations governing routine matters. (f) Supervision of instruction should be carried on through supervisors and principals under the leadership of the superintendent. The superintendent's leadership in supervision should be based upon a first-hand knowledge of conditions in the schools. (g) Textbooks and instructional supplies should be available through the superintendent or through an official who is responsible to him. (h) Enforcement of compulsory attendance laws should be under the direction of a chief attendance officer who is responsible to the superintendent. This official should have charge of the continuous school census. (i) Authorities having to do with buildings and grounds should center in the office of the superintendent of schools or in the office of the official who is responsible to the superintendent.[11]

It is important to note that Mr. Chamberlain says "that proper relation must be established between the superintendent and the school board and that responsibility must be definitely fixed," but he fails to show how either can be secured.

[11] Bennett C. Douglass. "The Status of the Superintendent." Department of Superintendence *First Yearbook*, 1: 4–152, 1923.

Dr. Theisen points out "that a board of education should endeavor to discover its own proper duties and those that should be delegated to professional executive officers." He makes it clear that a school board should determine the policies and that it is the function of the superintendent to execute the policies of the board. He emphasizes the principle that the board should always confine its work to seeing that the schools are properly administered. Never should the board itself administer the schools.

Dr. Morrison traces the development of the office of superintendent of schools and establishes the necessity for clear-cut definition of duties and responsibility in school administration.

Dr. Douglass summarizes the functions that boards of education and superintendents, respectively, most frequently initiate, execute, and approve; but he does not separate the functions that a board should perform from those that should be delegated to the employed chief executive.

THE PROBLEM

From the foregoing analysis, it is seen that at present no technique is available for determining the part a school board and its superintendent, respectively, should assume in handling the jobs and problems that occur in the administration of their school systems. It follows, then, that the purpose of this study is threefold: (1) to discover the functions a board of education should itself perform, (2) to determine the functions it should delegate to its employed professional chief executive and his subordinates, and (3) to ascertain how a board of education should do its work.

SOURCES OF DATA

This study is based chiefly on the jobs and problems which an analysis of school board minutes show have occurred during the last few years in thirteen cities. These cities range in population from approximately 5,000 to nearly a million, and are scattered through nine states from Kansas and Nebraska on the west to Rhode Island and Massachusetts on the east. Moreover, practically every type of school board organization and method of functioning was to be found in these cities during the period covered by the minutes studied. A list of the cities whose minutes form the basis of this study will be found in Appendix I.

METHODS USED

From the sources used and the type of problem, it follows that the methods used are mainly analytical and descriptive.

PROCEDURE

Step 1.—Establish criteria for determining the specific functions of a board of education.

Step 2.—Discover the specific jobs and problems that occur in administering school systems.

Step 3.—Group these jobs and problems under appropriate heads and subheads.

Step 4.—Analyze each job and problem to determine what the board of education itself should do in administering it and what tasks connected with it the school board should delegate to its superintendent of schools and his associates.

Step 5.—In the light of the best administrative theory and practice, and from the facts revealed and the conclusions drawn in *Steps* 1, 2, 3, and 4, ascertain how a board of education should do its work.

CRITERIA

As has been noted, the general functions of a board of education are now quite generally agreed upon. It follows, then, that the criteria for this study must grow out of, and be in accord with, those principles of educational administration which previous studies have evolved and which are commonly accepted by the profession as valid measures. To establish these criteria, it is proposed to consider various sources in the field of educational administration.

In his study,[12] Dr. Theisen set up these four criteria by which to measure the adequacy and correctness of a school board's functioning: "(1) use or waste of salaried professional skill actually purchased . . ., (2) economical use of time at the board's disposal, e.g., as represented by the distribution of time in board meetings . . . , (3) precision or definiteness, i.e., acting on adequate or in-

[12] William Walter Theisen. *The City Superintendent and the Board of Education.* Teachers College, Columbia University, VII ff, 1917.

adequate information in determining school policies as in such matters as the budget . . ., and (4) familiarity displayed by a board with its own actions." On the basis of these criteria, Dr. Theisen reached the conclusions and recommendations given on page 3 of this study.

Concerning his investigation of the administrative organization in the field of business and in the city manager form of commission government, Dr. Theisen reports as follows:

We found that each of these observes three fundamental principles of administration which permits of expert executive leadership: (1) A wide scope of authority is given to the chief executive in the control of other executives and in the direction of their duties. (2) As a counterpart to authority, responsibility for results is centered in the chief executive. The board of control retires from active administration but retains ultimate control through the budget and through reports that must be made showing the achievements, the business or financial status of the system. (3) In matters of policy the board of control demands that the chief executive and his assistants shall take the initiative. Expert leadership is purchased and utilized.[13]

Dr. Theisen then concludes that the same form of administrative organization and procedure should prevail in the field of public school administration. School superintendents, practical school board members, and authorities such as Strayer and Cubberley give utterance over and over to the fact that the work of a board of education is legislative and not executive.

Boards of education should act as legislative, and not as executive bodies, and a clear distinction should be drawn between what are legislative and what are executive functions. The legislative functions belong, by right, to the board, and the legislation should be enacted, after discussion, by means of formal and recorded votes. The board's work, as the representative of the people, is to sit in judgment on proposals and to determine the general policy of the school system.

Once a policy has been decided upon, however, its execution should rest with the executive officer or officers employed by the board, the chief of whom will naturally be the superintendent of schools.[14]

Probably the most important single matter that concerns the efficiency of a school system has to do with the determination and formulation of new policies which are established for the purpose of bringing about educational advancement. The superintendent is employed as the person presumably possessing the power to formulate such policies and one of his duties should be their presentation to the board of education for its consideration and

---

[13] *Ibid.*, p. 99 f.
[14] Ellwood P. Cubberley. *Public School Administration.* Houghton Mifflin Company. 1916, pp. 119 f.

approval. The board of education, as representing the people, must finally accept the responsibility for the adoption of any of these policies but not for their original formulation.[15]

Members of the board of education may best represent their constituency by selecting the highest type of executive that can be found. Having rendered this service they are under the obligation to require of him from time to time a record of the work done and proposals for the development of the school system placed in their charge. The executive, if he be competent, must make his case to the board of education, must be able to demonstrate the wisdom of the policies which he advocates, must be ready to defend in terms of a measurable achievement his own administration.[16]

Legislative, then, together with inspection of results, becomes the primary obligation of a board of education. . . . To legislate is to cause to be done; to execute is to do. To legislate is to set up policies which require action; to execute is to take the action necessary to the enforcement of the policy. . . . In the degree in which those who make policies undertake to do the work of executing them, which others ought to do, just in that degree do the policy makers assume responsibility for results.[17]

We must distinguish between the establishment of a policy and the administration of it. . . . When once established the carrying out of the policy is a function of the executive authority of the schools and must be carried out by the chief executive officer who is responsible for the execution and administration of all established policies.[18]

Dr. Betts pointed out that it is very doubtful if any unsalaried group of men or women in a school board will ever be willing to give permanent careful attention to details of public school administration. All that can be hoped from them is general supervision.[19]

On the character and ability of your superintendent depends the character and scope of your schools. In a city the size of ours, the trustees can do but little toward supervising,—they can only pass on expenditures, legislate, and advise.[20]

The general functions of a board of education may then be summarized as follows: (1) Select the superintendent of schools. (2) Determine the policies of the school system. (3) See that these policies are carried out by the superintendent and his associates.

Now, if a valid definition of policy can be established, it will

---

[15] Charles E. Chadsey. "The Report of the Committee on the Status of the Superintendent." Department of Superintendence, *First Yearbook*, 1923, 157 f.

[16] George D. Strayer. "The Relation of Administrative Officers to Boards of Education." N. E. A. Department of Superintendence *First Yearbook*, 1923, p. 160.

[17] J. W. Studebaker (Superintendent of Schools, Des Moines, Iowa). "School Board Organization and the Superintendent." Address delivered before The Department of Superintendence of the National Education Association at Chicago in 1924 and published in *American School Board Journal*, 68: 38 f, April, 1924.

[18] Fred M. Hunter (Superintendent of Schools, Oakland, California). "Professional Leadership of Superintendent." *American Educational Digest*, 44: 292, March, 1925.

[19] Report of address by Dr. F. W. Betts, Chairman of Syracuse (New York) School Committee delivered before that body, *American Educational Digest*, 44: 303 f, March, 1925.

[20] R. D. Benson (President of Board of Education, Passaic, New Jersey), in a supplementary report to the board, which on a unanimous vote was incorporated in the minutes and a copy given to the press. Passaic, January 27, 1920.

be perfectly feasible to segregate the work of the school board from that of its employed chief executive. And if this can be done, it follows that the "means of establishing definite working relations between school boards and superintendents" is available.

Analysis of the word "policy" as it is used in the field of administration reveals that it is intended to signify a decision, or set of decisions, whether definitely formulated or not, as to how given problems and jobs shall be solved and administered. The term "administrative detail," on the other hand, invariably has reference to a single case or some aspect of an individual case. The two criteria, therefore, that are to be applied in this study may be expressed as follows:

Decisions determining how problems and jobs shall be solved and administered are policies.

Application of policies to single or individual problems and jobs is an administrative detail.

A major function of this study, then, is to apply these two definitions, as criteria, to the problems and jobs that occur in administering school systems and by that means determine the exact part a school board and its superintendent, respectively, should play in meeting the jobs and problems as they occur in the administration of their school system. This will be done in Chapter II.

If these criteria are accepted by a board of education, it follows that the board will seldom, if ever, concern itself with specific or individual cases. Instead, it will determine the policies that shall govern in administering single cases. Should a case arise for which there is no established policy, the superintendent will rarely take this case to the board for its consideration. On the contrary, he will analyze the case to determine the issue upon which a decision by the board is needed, and it will be the function of the board to establish its policy with respect to this issue. After such action has been taken by the board, the superintendent will apply the policy to the particular case in question. This whole problem of how the board should function will be discussed in Chapter III.

DIVISIONS OF THE STUDY

Chapter I has set up the problem and the technique that will be used in its solution. In Chapter II the jobs and problems occurring in the administering of school systems will be analyzed, and the respective functions of the school board and its chief executive will be set forth. Chapter III will be devoted to the problem of how the board of education should do its work.

CHAPTER II

SCHOOL BOARDS AND SUPERINTENDENTS: THEIR WORK

A careful analysis of previous studies in the field reveals, as is shown in Chapter I, that while the board of education is to determine the policies of the school district, it is not the function of the school board itself to do the research and study necessary to arrive at the decisions that are to be its policies. Instead, as Dr. Chadsey points out, "The superintendent is employed as the person presumably possessing the power to formulate such policies, and one of his duties should be their presentation to the board of education for its consideration and approval."[1] Hence, before presenting the analysis of problems and jobs occurring in public school administration, it is appropriate to make clear by means of analogy the respective functions of a school board and its superintendent in the matter of policy determination.

According to previous studies and as is shown in Chapter I, the superintendent of schools bears a relationship to the board of education that is closely analogous to that of a physician to the parents of a child who is his patient. The physician is the expert professional health adviser of the parents. It is presumed that by virtue of his training and experience the physician is an authority on matters of health. But even so, it is for the parents to decide whether or not the advice of this expert is to be followed.

If for some reason the parents lose faith in their medical adviser, they will not set out to study medicine in order to determine how their ailing child should be treated. Instead, they will call in other physicians—experts in the science of healing—and have them verify the conclusions and recommendations of their own physician.

Should the consulting physicians concur in the diagnosis and recommendations of the family physician, the parents are still free to accept or reject the combined judgment of the physicians

[1] Charles E. Chadsey. "The Report of the Committee on the Status of the Superintendent." N. E. A. Department of Superintendence *First Yearbook*, 157 f, 1923.

11

as a basis for action. They may agree with the experts that a trip to Florida would be beneficial, and yet conclude that the cost of the trip makes it prohibitive or otherwise undesirable. They may agree with the medical experts that an operation is needed; but because they feel that the risk involved is too great, they may decide to have the child continue under the physical handicap rather than have it submit to the operation.

In school administration, the school district corresponds to the child in the foregoing analogy; the superintendent corresponds to the physician; and the board of education corresponds to the parents. In passing upon the issues that it must consider in determining its policies, the board of education should always proceed as would the parents in this analogy. If it does not have confidence in its superintendent, it should call in other experts in the field of school administration. In no case, should the board itself attempt to do the work of the expert. But the board of education should always approve or reject the recommendations of the superintendent and of the consulting experts it may employ.

The Work of School Boards and Superintendents Differentiated

In this chapter will be presented, on the basis of criteria previously set up, an analysis of the problems and jobs found to occur in administering more than a dozen public school systems. In each of these problems and jobs, the work of the board of education will be definitely separated from that of its employed chief executive and his associates.

It is freely admitted that a school board has the legal right and authority to assume any and all of the work connected with the numerous problems and jobs occurring in the administration of its school system. In Chapter III, however, it will be shown that for a board to attempt to perform other work than that assigned it in this chapter leads to inefficient administration and to divided responsibility.

The amount of space devoted to the respective problems and jobs is no indication of their relative importance. Neither is the varying number of issues raised under each so to be considered. The amount of space given and the number of issues raised merely mean that to analyze adequately each problem and job, the author has found this space and these issues necessary.

No claim is made that all problems and jobs occurring in administering a system of public schools are here listed and analyzed. Neither is it believed that here is raised every possible issue under each problem and job. This study presents a careful analysis of by far the major portion of the work of public school administration, and it suggests how other problems and jobs may be treated when they arise.

PROBLEM OR JOB: THE WORK OF THE PUBLIC SCHOOLS

Decisions made by a board of education on these and like issues are its policies:

1. What services shall the public schools render to
   a. Persons of compulsory school age; if they are
      1) Normal children?
      2) Subnormal children?
      3) Superior children?
      4) Blind children?
      5) Deaf children?
      6) Crippled children?
      7) Tubercular children?
      8) Delinquent children?
   b. Persons of pre-school age, if they are
      1) Normal children?
      2) Subnormal children?
      3) Superior children?
      4) Blind children?
      5) Deaf children?
      6) Crippled children?
      7) Tubercular children?
   c. Persons past the compulsory school age in the form of
      1) Extension courses?
      2) Lectures?
      3) Americanization work?
      4) Health clinic?
      5) Recreation facilities?
2. Annual appropriations:
   a. What shall be the annual appropriation for each service the public schools render the respective groups?

Administrative Jobs

These and like administrative jobs should be delegated to the superintendent of schools:

1. Collect and organize adequate data for the board intelligently to determine the services the schools should render each group and the annual appropriation that should be made for each activity.

2. Provide for each group the services that the board of education decides the public schools should render it.

3. Keep adequate records of the services rendered each group and make appropriate reports of it to the board of education.

PROBLEM OR JOB: THE CURRICULUM

Decisions made by a board of education on these and like issues are its policies:

Courses and Subjects

1. To be offered:
    a. What courses and subjects shall be taught in the respective divisions and grades of the school system?
    b. What courses and subjects shall be taught pupils who because of illness or other physical incapacity are unable to come to the public school buildings?
    c. What school-home projects shall the public schools carry on?
    d. What courses shall be presented to satisfy college entrance requirements?
    e. What shall be the minimum number of pupils for which a course or class shall be conducted?
2. For whom offered:
    a. To whom shall each class and course be open?
    b. Under what conditions shall the qualifications for admission to the different courses and classes be changed?
3. Content:
    a. What shall be the content of the respective courses and subjects?
    b. Where there is more than one system of a subject (shorthand and penmanship, for example), what system shall be taught?

c. How and to what extent shall requests and communications from non-school groups be permitted to influence the content of courses?

d. Under what conditions may prizes from private individuals or non-school organizations be offered for work in the public schools?

e. May non-school groups initiate and foster contests in the public schools? If so,
   1) What types of contests may be conducted by them or through their aid?
   2) How shall such contests be conducted?

f. Suppose strong criticism against a course comes from either patrons or pupils, or both. How shall such criticism be met (i.e., shall the course be continued as it is, be reorganized, or be discontinued)?

g. How shall demands of taxpayers, parents, and others for curtailments of activities in the curriculum be met?

h. Shall non-school organizations be invited to give or be permitted to present courses to either children or adults under the auspices of the public schools?

i. If so, under what conditions may such courses be offered?

j. May non-school groups or organizations have the use of rooms in public school buildings for the purpose of presenting to public school pupils courses supplementing or not included in the public school curriculum?

k. May the industrial arts department construct projects or make repairs either for the schools or for non-school groups? If so, on what conditions?

l. May the home economics department serve luncheons and banquets for either school or non-school groups? If so, on what conditions?

m. What charges may a department make for such services?

n. How shall the money so earned be used?

o. May discussions on subjects not included in the regular courses be held in class recitations or in other sessions during the school day?

p. What subjects may not be discussed?

q. Shall courses in normal training, agriculture, home economics, etc., conform with the requirements necessary to receive state and federal aid?

     r. Shall courses be submitted to and be approved by the state department of education?

     s. To what degree shall the content of courses be made to conform with the entrance requirements of colleges and universities?

4. Credit:

     a. What credit shall be offered in the respective courses and subjects?

     b. Shall credit be given for work done by non-school groups outside of the public schools? For example, shall credit be given for out-of-school Bible study?

5. Required and elective:

     a. What courses shall be compulsory?

     b. What courses shall be elective?

     c. What shall be the pupil's distribution of time among the different courses and subjects?

6. Results:

     a. What shall be the results or standards of achievements in the respective courses and subjects?

     b. What exhibits may be made of the work done in the public schools?

     c. How much money shall be appropriated annually for such exhibits?

7. Revisions:

     a. What studies shall be carried on to determine the appropriateness of the contents of the different courses and subjects in the curriculum?

     b. What annual appropriation shall be made for curriculum reconstruction research?

     c. What curriculum revisions shall be made?

8. Fees:

     a. What fees shall be required of pupils taking the different courses?

     b. Under what conditions shall such fees be refunded?

Administrative Jobs

These and like administrative jobs should be delegated to the superintendent of schools:

1. Collect and organize adequate data for the board to determine intelligently its policy on each issue.

2. Keep the public adequately informed in regard to the subjects and courses included in the public school curriculum.
3. Prepare the courses.
4. Carry on curriculum reconstruction research.
5. Revise and reorganize the courses.
6. Receive and evaluate requests for changes in the curriculum.
7. Admit and assign pupils to courses.
8. Transfer pupils from course to course.
9. Certify and issue credits to pupils.
10. Provide the courses authorized.
11. Exclude prohibited matter from courses.
12. Make the courses satisfy such requirements of the state department, entrance requirements of colleges and universities, and requirements for state and federal aid as the policies of the school board demand.
13. Determine the results in the different courses.
14. Prepare exhibits of the school work and properly display them.
15. Determine methods of teaching to be used in the different subjects and courses.
16. Receive requests that contests be conducted in the public schools.
17. Grant or deny such requests.
18. Conduct contests.
19. Receive offers to donate prizes.
20. Accept or refuse such offers.
21. Award prizes.
22. Receive requests for and authorize projects and repairs that industrial arts department may make.
23. Receive requests for and authorize luncheons and banquets that home economics department may serve.
24. Collect the charges to be made for such services by these departments.
25. Assign courses and grades to rooms and buildings.
26. Transfer courses and grades from room to room and from building to building.
27. Collect fees.
28. Refund fees.

Problem or Job: LIBRARIES

Decisions made by a board of education on these and like issues are its policies:

1. Facilities:
   a. What library facilities shall be provided in the different schools?
   b. Shall rooms be furnished in public school buildings for branch public libraries or for community libraries?
2. Books, magazines, etc.:
   a. What kinds or types of books, magazines, etc., may not be placed in school libraries?
3. Appropriations:
   a. What shall be the annual appropriation for school libraries?
4. Aid from individual schools or school communities:
   a. Shall the respective schools or school communities match the amounts provided by the district for school libraries?
5. Loss of libraries:
   a. Suppose a school library provided by an organization such as parent-teacher association is destroyed, shall the district reimburse the organization for such loss?

Administrative Jobs

These and like administrative jobs should be delegated to the superintendent of schools:

1. Ascertain library facilities needed in each school.
2. Determine appropriation needed for library purposes during the year.
3. Assign rooms for library purposes.
4. Select and purchase magazines, books, and other publications for libraries in accordance with the policies of the school board.
5. Collect from each school the amount it must contribute to school libraries.
6. Reimburse organizations contributing to school libraries in accordance with the policies of the board of education.
7. Keep adequate records of all matters pertaining to school libraries and submit suitable reports thereof to the board of education.

PROBLEM OR JOB: HEALTH SERVICE

Decisions made by a board of education on these and like issues are its policies:

1. Clinics:
   a. Shall the district establish and maintain
      1) Dental clinics?
      2) Baby clinics?
   b. What services shall such clinics render, and to whom?
   c. What charges shall such clinics make for the services they render?
2. Physical examinations:
   a. What physical examinations shall be made of public school pupils?
   b. When and by whom shall such examinations be made?
   c. What use shall be made of the findings of such examinations?
3. Health programs:
   a. How and to what extent shall the schools endorse and support a community health program?
4. Volunteer health work?
   a. Shall volunteer health workers be given recognition by the school district in order that their work may be more effective?
5. Corrective work:
   a. What corrective work shall be provided public school pupils?
6. Vaccinations and tests:
   a. Shall vaccination of pupils be compulsory?
   b. On what conditions may exemption from vaccination be granted?
   c. What shall be the penalty for failure to comply with regulations pertaining to vaccination?
   d. Shall the district recommend or require the application to school children of such tests as the Shick and the Dick tests?
   e. Under what conditions shall the district provide vaccinations, Dick tests, and Shick tests to public school pupils?
7. Distribution of health literature:
   a. What kinds of health pamphlets and bulletins may be distributed in the public schools?

  b. At what times and under what conditions may such literature be distributed?
8. Exclusion of pupils:
  a. What symptoms of illness shall exclude pupils from school?
  b. What records shall be made of such symptoms when pupils are excluded?
  c. How shall pupils developing symptoms of illness in school be sent home?
9. How may medical associations, dental associations, parent-teacher associations, nurses associations, foundations, the Red Cross, etc., coöperate with the school district in conducting its health service?
10. Appropriations:
  a. What shall be the annual appropriation for the district's health service?

Administrative Jobs

These and like administrative jobs should be delegated to the superintendent of schools:
1. Establish clinics.
2. See that each clinic provides the services for which it is maintained.
3. Collect appropriate charges for services rendered.
4. Have physical examinations made.
5. Use findings of such examinations as directed by the board of education.
6. Conduct health programs.
7. Give such official recognition to volunteer health workers as the policies of the board of education require.
8. Provide corrective health work.
9. Have vaccinations, Shick tests, Dick tests, etc., made as required by the board of education.
10. Exempt pupils from vaccinations and such tests.
11. Enforce penalties for failure to comply with regulations pertaining to vaccinations and such tests.
12. Distribute health literature.
13. Exclude ailing pupils.
14. Make and keep the required records of pupils excluded because of illness.

15. Coöperate with non-school agencies in conducting the health service of the district and the community.
16. Determine the appropriation needed annually for carrying on the school health service.
17. Keep adequate records of all matters pertaining to health service and submit appropriate reports thereof to the board of education.

PROBLEM OR JOB: MILK FOR PUBLIC SCHOOL PUPILS

Decisions made by a board of education on these and like issues are its policies:

1. How furnished:
    a. Shall such organizations as the Red Cross, the Visiting Nurses Association, and Parent-Teacher Associations be requested or permitted to serve milk free of charge or at cost to:
       1) All pupils?
       2) Undernourished pupils?
       3) Underweight pupils?
    b. Shall the district furnish milk free or at cost to each of above groups of pupils?
2. Appropriations:
    a. What shall be the annual appropriation for milk for public school pupils?

Administrative Jobs

These and like administrative jobs should be delegated to the superintendent of schools:

1. Have milk served in public schools in accordance with policies of the board of education.
2. Make arrangements for coöperation with non-school agencies in this work.
3. Purchase and distribute the milk required.
4. Pay for milk purchased.
5. Ascertain the annual appropriation needed for milk.
6. Keep the necessary records pertaining to the supplying of milk to public school pupils and submit the proper reports thereof to the school board.

PROBLEM OR JOB: CAFETERIAS AND LUNCHROOMS

Decisions made by a board of education on these and like issues are its policies:

1. Cafeteria and lunchroom facilities:
    a. What cafeteria and lunchroom facilities shall be provided in the different schools for each of the following?
        1) All pupils
        2) Undernourished pupils
        3) Underweight pupils
        4) Blind pupils
        5) Pupils in sight-saving classes
        6) Crippled pupils
        7) Tubercular pupils
2. Meals served:
    a. What meals shall be served each of the above groups of pupils?
    b. Shall such meals be served each of the above groups—
        1) Free?
        2) At less than cost?
        3) At a profit?
        4) At cost?
    c. Shall such organizations as the Red Cross, the Visiting Nurses Association, and Parent-Teacher Associations be requested or be permitted to coöperate with the public schools in serving meals to one or more of the above groups of pupils?
3. Management:
    a. Shall cafeterias and lunchrooms be operated by the district or by outside agencies?
    b. If outside agencies are to operate them, what shall be the bases for selecting such agencies?
    c. To what rules and regulations shall outside agencies operating cafeterias and lunchrooms conform?
    d. What shall be the remuneration of such outside agencies?
    e. What supervision of pupils shall be provided in cafeterias and dining rooms?
4. Appropriations:
    a. What shall be the annual appropriation for cafeterias and lunchrooms?

Administrative Jobs

These and like administrative jobs should be delegated to the superintendent of schools:

1. Ascertain cafeteria and lunchroom facilities needed.
2. Advise the board of education as to the meals that should be served.
3. Make recommendations to the school board as to the desirable methods of operating cafeterias and lunchrooms.
4. Operate these in accordance with the policies of the board.
5. Supervise operation of lunchrooms and cafeterias when these are conducted by outside agencies.
6. Remunerate such outside agencies as the policies of the board require.
7. Supervise pupils in cafeterias and lunchrooms.
8. Ascertain the annual appropriation needed for cafeterias and lunchrooms.
9. Keep suitable records of all matters pertaining to cafeterias and lunchrooms and submit appropriate reports thereof to the board of education.

PROBLEM OR JOB: RECREATION AND PLAY

Decisions made by a board of education on these and like issues are its policies:

1. Program:
   a. What program of recreation and play shall be provided for public school pupils?
   b. Shall separate recreational play facilities be provided for colored pupils?
2. Coöperation with non-school organizations:
   a. How shall the public schools coöperate with non-school agencies in promoting the school recreation and play program?
3. Appropriations:
   a. What shall be the annual appropriation for the recreation and play program?

Administrative Jobs

These and like administrative jobs should be delegated to the superintendent of schools:

1. Advise the board of education as to an appropriate program of recreation and play.
2. Ascertain the appropriation needed annually for carrying on such a program.
3. Coöperate as required by the policies of the school board, with non-school agencies in promoting the school recreation and play program.
4. See that the school recreation and play program functions as it should.
5. Keep adequate records of the recreation and play program and keep the board of education duly informed thereon.

———

PROBLEM OR JOB: THE ATHLETIC PROGRAM

Decisions made by a board of education on these and like issues are its policies:

1. Annual athletic program:
   a. What shall be the annual athletic program?
   b. What sports shall the schools foster?
   c. Which of these sports shall be carried on in interschool contests?
   d. Which of these sports shall be conducted only as intramural sports?
   e. How many contest games in each sport may be scheduled during the year?
2. Annual appropriations for athletics:
   a. What shall be the amount appropriated annually for athletics?
   b. What amount shall be appropriated annually for each sport?
3. Expenditures for athletics:
   a. What may be the total annual expenditures for athletics?
   b. What part of the annual expenditures for athletics shall be devoted to each sport fostered?

Administrative Jobs

These and like administrative jobs should be delegated to the superintendent of schools:

1. Advise the board of education as to the desirability of a given athletic program.

2. Carry out the athletic program adopted by the board of education.
3. Determine the amount necessary to conduct the athletic program adopted by the board of education.
4. See that the appropriations and expenditures for athletics are made in accordance with the policies of the board of education.
5. Keep adequate records of all matters pertaining to athletics and submit reports thereof to the board of education.

PROBLEM OR JOB: CONTROL OF ATHLETICS

Decisions made by a board of education on these and like issues are its policies:

1. Membership in district and state athletic associations:
    a. Shall the respective schools of the system be members of the district and state athletic associations?
    b. Shall the schools abide by the rules and regulations of such athletic associations?
    c. Suppose one of the schools within the system is suspended or expelled from the district or the state athletic association for any reason. What shall be done about it?
2. Student athletic associations:
    a. May pupils in the different schools of the system form athletic associations?
    b. To whom shall membership in such athletic associations be open?
    c. What control of athletics may such associations have?
    d. May such athletic associations select and pay coaches with or without the active supervision of the school authorities?
3. Qualifications of participants in interschool contests:
    a. What shall be the qualifications of individuals participating in interschool contests?
4. Number of interschool contests:
    a. In how many interschool contests may each school participate each year?
5. School time devoted to practice, trips, and contests:
    a. How much school time may be devoted to practice for interschool contests?

    b. How much school time may be used by teams in making trips to contests away from home?

    c. May athletic contests be played during school hours?

6. Dismissal of school for athletic contests:

    a. If athletic contests are played during school hours, shall school be dismissed in order that pupils not participating in the contests may attend them?

7. Attendance of non-participating pupils at games away from home:

    a. When interschool contests are played away from home, may non-participating pupils be excused from school to attend such contests?

8. Practice while schools closed:

    a. May practice for athletic contests go on while schools are closed by order of the board of health?

9. Practice on Sundays and holidays:

    a. May practice for athletic contests be permitted on Sundays and holidays?

10. Exhibition games:

    a. May school teams play exhibition games?

    b. If so, under what conditions?

Administrative Jobs

These and like administrative jobs should be delegated to the superintendent of schools:

1. Secure and maintain membership in district and state athletic associations.

2. Enforce the rules and regulations of such organizations.

3. In case of suspension or expulsion from such associations, secure reinstatement.

4. Organize and supervise student athletic associations.

5. Arrange for and schedule interschool contests in accordance with the policies of the school board.

6. Select pupils to participate in athletic contests.

7. Supervise such contests.

8. Supervise trips to contests and chaperon pupils on trips.

9. Schedule time for practice for interschool contests.

10. Supervise such practice.

11. Dismiss school for interschool athletic contests in accordance with policies of the board of education.

12. Excuse non-participating pupils in order that they may attend athletic contests away from home.
13. Schedule and supervise exhibition games in accordance with the rules and regulations of the school board.
14. Keep adequate records of all matters pertaining to the control of athletics and submit suitable reports thereof to the board of education.

PROBLEM OR JOB: FINANCING OF ATHLETICS

Decisions made by a board of education on these and like issues are its policies:

1. Appropriations:
   a. What shall be the annual appropriation for athletics?
2. How financed:
   a. By taxation?
   b. By donations from outside organizations and private individuals?
   c. By contributions from school organizations?
   d. By subscriptions from individual pupils?
   e. By gate receipts?
      1) Single and season tickets to pupils?
      2) Single and season tickets to the general public?
   f. By two or more of these methods?
3. Annual expenditures for athletics:
   a. What shall be the maximum amount that may be expended for athletics in any school year?
4. Loans to student organizations:
   a. Shall the school authorities make loans to student athletic organizations in order that such organizations may carry on athletic programs?
5. Deficits of student athletic associations:
   a. Shall the school authorities make up deficits incurred by student athletic associations?
6. Gate receipts:
   a. What admission shall be charged to athletic contests?
   b. For what purposes may the proceeds from athletic contests be used?
7. Athletic funds:
   a. How and by whom shall athletic funds be handled?

Administrative Jobs

These and like administrative jobs should be delegated to the superintendent of schools:

1. Determine the amount of money necessary to conduct the annual program of athletics.
2. See to it that the amount authorized for athletics by the board of education is raised.
3. Expend the athletic funds in accordance with the rules of the board of education.
4. Make loans to student athletic associations as the policies of the board require.
5. Secure payment of such loans.
6. Determine the validity of deficits of student athletic associations and reimburse such organizations for these deficits as the policies of the school board demand.
7. Collect admissions at the gate.
8. Properly allocate all athletic receipts and place them in the appropriate funds.
9. Establish and maintain an appropriate system of accounting of athletic funds.
10. Make suitable reports on the financing of athletics to the board of education.

PROBLEM OR JOB: PROMOTION OF ATHLETICS BY NON-SCHOOL AGENCIES

Decisions made by a board of education on these and like issues are its policies:

1. May non-school agencies promote school athletics by
   a. Money contributions?
   b. Providing coaches?
   c. Providing athletic fields or stadia?
   d. Offering pennants, trophies, trips to tournaments?
2. Under what conditions may such aid for athletics be received?

Administrative Jobs

These and like administrative jobs should be delegated to the superintendent of schools:

1. Receive offers of aid for school athletics.

2. Accept or reject such offers in accordance with the policies of the board of education.
3. Use accepted aid as the rules of the board of education require.

PROBLEM OR JOB: COACHES OF ATHLETICS

Decisions made by a board of education on these and like issues are its policies:

1. Qualifications:
    a. What shall be the qualifications of coaches of the respective sports?
    (Note: See Qualifications of Instructional Staff, page 73.)
2. Salary schedule:
    a. What shall be the salary schedule of coaches?
3. Number of coaches:
    a. Shall each sport be provided with a special coach?
    b. What shall be the total number of coaches employed for athletics?
4. Relation of coaches to one another:
    a. What shall be the relation of coaches to one another?
        1) In the same sport?
        2) In different sports?
5. Relation of coaches to the director of physical education and the principal:
    a. What shall be the relation of coaches to the director of of physical education and to the principal of the school?
6. Coaches for colored teams:
    a. Shall colored teams be provided with coaches?
7. Appropriations:
    a. What shall be the annual appropriations for coaches?
8. Selection of coaches:
    a. May pupils or non-school agencies select and pay the coaches with or without the approval of the superintendent?

Administrative Jobs

These and like administrative jobs should be delegated to the superintendent of schools:

1. Select coaches.

2. Employ coaches.
3. Suspend or ask for the resignation of coaches.
4. Pay coaches.
5. Assign coaches.
6. Reassign coaches.
7. See to it that the proper relationship is maintained among coaches.
8. See to it that the right relation between coaches and the director of physical education is maintained.

PROBLEM OR JOB: MANAGER OF ATHLETICS

Decisions made by a board of education on these and like issues are its policies:

1. Employment:
   a. Shall a manager of athletics be employed?
   b. Shall there be one manager of athletics or shall there be a different manager for each of the sports fostered by the schools?
2. Qualifications:
   a. What shall be the qualifications of a manager of athletics?
3. Duties and responsibilities:
   a. What shall be the duties and responsibilities of a manager of athletics?
4. Relation to coaches, director of physical education, and principal:
   a. What shall be the relation of the manager of athletics to the coaches, to the director of physical education, and to the principal of the school?
5. Salary:
   a. What shall be the salary schedule of the manager of athletics?
6. Appropriations:
   a. What shall be annual appropriation for managers of athletics?

Administrative Jobs

These and like administrative jobs should be delegated to the superintendent of schools:

1. Select manager of athletics.

2. Employ managers.
3. Suspend or ask for the resignation of managers.
4. Pay managers.
5. Assign managers.
6. Reassign managers.
7. See to it that the right relations prevail between managers and coaches.

PROBLEM OR JOB: ACCIDENTS IN ATHLETICS

Decisions made by a board of education on these and like issues are its policies:

1. Physicians at contests:
   a. Shall physicians for accident emergencies be employed to attend athletic contests?
   b. What shall be the pay of such physicians?
2. Medical attention in dressing rooms:
   a. Shall medical aid be available in dressing rooms for ministering to sprains and bruises of pupils participating in athletics?
   b. What amount shall be appropriated for this purpose?
3. Reimbursement of pupils for expenditures incurred as result of injuries:
   a. Shall the school district reimburse pupils for doctor bills, hospital bills, dental bills, and nurse bills incurred as a result of exposure or injuries received in athletic activities fostered by the schools?
   b. What amount shall be appropriated for this purpose?

Administrative Jobs

These and like administrative jobs should be delegated to the superintendent of schools:

1. Provide such physicians and medical attention for pupils participating in school athletics as the policies of the board of education require.
2. Pay such physicians.
3. Keep adequate records of such expenditures and make appropriate reports thereof to the board of education.

PROBLEM OR JOB: INSURANCE OF ATHLETIC CONTESTS, PARTICIPANTS, AND SPECTATORS

Decisions made by a board of education on these and like issues are its policies:

1. Insurance against loss due to storms, etc.:
    a. If admissions are charged to athletic contests, shall insurance be taken out to cover financial losses incurred by weather conditions, etc.?
2. Insurance of participants in contests:
    a. Shall the school district carry insurance against accidents and death of participants in athletic contests?
3. Insurance of spectators:
    a. Shall the school district carry insurance against injury and death of spectators at athletic contests?
4. Amount of insurance:
    a. What amount of insurance shall the school district carry for each of these risks?
5. Placement of insurance:
    a. What shall be the qualifications of the companies with which such insurance is placed?

Administrative Jobs

These and like administrative jobs should be delegated to the superintendent of schools:

1. Place such insurance as the policies of the board require and with such companies as satisfy the qualifications specified by the board of education.
2. Pay premiums on such insurance.
3. Collect insurance on such policies and see to it that it is paid to the proper persons or funds.

PROBLEM OR JOB: ATHLETIC HONORS AND TROPHIES

Decisions made by a board of education on these and like issues are its policies:

1. Honors:
    a. What honors shall be bestowed upon pupils participating in athletic contests?
    b. May members of school athletic teams receive presents

and banquet honors from non-school agencies in recognition of their athletic ability and services?

   c. On what basis shall honor awards in athletics be granted?

2. Athletic trophies:

   a. What shall be the maximum value of an athletic trophy which may be awarded?

   b. Under what conditions shall athletic trophies be awarded?

   c. Who may provide athletic trophies?

   d. Under what conditions?

Administrative Jobs

These and like administrative jobs should be delegated to the superintendent of schools:

1. Purchase athletic honors (sweaters, letters, etc.).
2. Award such honors.
3. Present these honors.
4. Purchase trophies.
5. Receive or reject offers of trophies.
6. Award trophies.
7. Present trophies.

Problem or Job: ATHLETIC TOURNAMENTS

Decisions made by a board of education on these and like issues are its policies:

1. Participation in tournaments:

   a. May the teams of the respective schools in the system participate in tournaments?

   b. May the teams in tournaments compete with non-school or professional teams?

2. Appropriations for tournaments:

   a. What shall be the annual appropriation for trips to tournaments?

3. Expenditures for tournaments:

   a. May the expenditures for trips to tournaments exceed the appropriations allowed by the board of education for this purpose?

   b. If so, under what conditions?

Administrative Jobs

These and like administrative jobs should be delegated to the superintendent of schools:

1. Enter teams for participation in tournaments as the policies of the board of education permit or require.
2. Supervise trips to tournaments and chaperon pupils making such trips.
3. Determine the appropriations necessary for making trips to tournaments.
4. Make expenditures for trips to tournaments as the policies of the board of education demand.
5. Keep adequate records of matters pertaining to tournaments and submit appropriate reports thereof to the board of education.

PROBLEM OR JOB: ATHLETIC FIELDS' AND STADIA

Decisions made by a board of education on these and like issues are its policies:

1. Purchase or lease of sites:
   a. Shall sites for athletic fields be purchased or leased?
2. Selection of sites:
   a. What sites shall be purchased or leased for athletic purposes?
3. Cost of sites:
   a. What sums shall be paid for sites or for rent of sites to be used for athletic fields?
4. Improvement of sites:
   a. How much shall be expended for putting each athletic site in shape for an athletic field?
5. Maintenance of athletic fields:
   a. How much shall be expended annually for the maintenance of athletic fields?
6. Construction of stadia and grand stands:
   a. Shall a stadium or grand stand be constructed?
   b. At what cost?
7. Sources of funds used for athletic fields and stadia:
   a. From what sources shall money for athletic fields and stadia be secured?
   1) Subscriptions from the public?

     2) Alumni drives?

     3) Taxation?

8. Maintenance of stadia and grand stands:

   a. How much shall be expended annually for the maintenance of stadia and grand stands?

9. Appropriations for athletic fields and stadia:

   a. What shall be the annual appropriation for athletic fields and stadia?

10. Use of athletic fields:

   a. For what sports:

     1) May an athletic field be used for a purpose other than for the specific sports for which it is constructed?

   b. By non-school groups:

     1) What non-school groups may use athletic fields when these are not used by the schools?

     2) May non-school groups have the use of athletic fields on Sundays?

     3) What shall determine the rent that non-school groups shall pay for the use of athletic fields?

     4) Shall non-school groups be required to make advance deposits to cover possible damages to fields while these are leased to them?

     5) What shall be the amounts of such deposits?

11. Policing of athletic fields:

   a. How shall the athletic fields be policed during the time they are used

     1) By the schools?

     2) By non-school groups?

12. Allocation of income from athletic fields:

   a. Into what funds shall money be placed that is collected for the use of or for damage done to athletic fields?

Administrative Jobs

These and like administrative jobs should be delegated to the superintendent of schools:

1. Advise the board of education as to the desirability of proposed sites for athletic fields.

2. Purchase sites for athletic fields.

3. Pay for sites for athletic fields.

4. Plan and build athletic fields on new sites.

5. Employ and pay the necessary help to build such athletic fields.
6. Purchase the material necessary for the building of athletic fields and pay for same.
7. Keep the athletic fields in condition for the sports for which they are to be used.
8. Plan and build stadia and grand stands.
9. Employ and pay the necessary help to build stadia and grand stands.
10. Purchase and pay for material necessary for stadia and grand stands.
11. Keep stadia and grand stands in repair.
12. Secure the money for athletic fields, stadia, and grand stands from the sources designated by the board of education.
13. Advise the board of education as to the annual appropriations required for athletic fields and stadia.
14. See to it that the athletic fields are used for the sports for which they are maintained and for no others.
15. Lease athletic fields to non-school groups in accordance with the policies of the school board.
16. Collect rent from non-school groups for the use of athletic fields.
17. Collect advance deposits from non-school groups using athletic fields.
18. Make adjustments for damages done athletic fields, stadia, and grand stands while these are leased to non-school groups.
19. Collect such damages from non-school groups.
20. Refund deposits made by non-school groups using athletic fields as required by the policies of the board of education.
21. Place all money collected from non-school groups for the use of or damage to athletic fields in the funds designated by the board of education.
22. See to it that the athletic fields are properly policed as required by the rules of the school board.
23. Keep adequate records of all matters pertaining to athletic fields and stadia and submit suitable reports thereof to the board of education.

PROBLEM OR JOB: ALUMNI AND FORMER STUDENTS

Decisions made by a board of education on these and like issues are its policies:

1. Services:
   a. What services shall the schools render alumni and former students?
   b. Shall these services be rendered without cost to alumni and former students?
2. Records of:
   a. What records shall be kept of alumni and former students?
3. Successes and failures:
   a. Shall alumni and former students be followed up to learn their successes and failures in an effort to discover the efficiency of the training received by them in the public schools?
4. Appropriations:
   a. What shall be the annual appropriation for carrying on work with alumni and former students?

Administrative Jobs

These and like administrative jobs should be delegated to the superintendent of schools:

1. Provide such services for alumni and former students as the policies of the board require.
2. Establish and develop such follow-up work of alumni and former students as the board may authorize.
3. Ascertain the annual appropriation required for work with alumni and former students.
4. Develop and keep appropriate records of alumni and former students.
5. Submit suitable reports to the board of education on all matters pertaining to alumni and former students.

PROBLEM OR JOB: STUDENT PUBLICATIONS

Decisions made by a board of education on these and like issues are its policies:

1. Kind and number:
   a. What papers, magazines, bulletins, annuals, etc., may the pupils of the respective schools publish?

2. Name:
   a. What shall be the names of such publications?
3. Content:
   a. What shall be the content of each of these publications?
4. Frequency of issue:
   a. At what intervals may such publications be issued?
5. Printing:
   a. Shall the printing of such publications be done by the pupils as projects in the school print shops?
   b. If the printing is done by commercial printers, what shall be the qualifications of printers by whom this work may be done?
6. Cost:
   a. How shall the cost of such publications be borne?
7. Appropriations:
   a. What shall be the annual appropriation for such publications?

Administrative Jobs

These and like administrative jobs should be delegated to the superintendent of schools:

1. Supervise the publication of such student magazines, bulletins, annuals, etc., as the policies of the board permit or require.
2. Ascertain the annual appropriation needed for such student publications.
3. Keep adequate records of all matters pertaining to such publications and submit suitable reports thereof to the board of education.

Problem or Job: SPECIAL INSTRUCTION FOR HANDI-CAPPED PUPILS

Decisions made by a board of education on these and like issues are its policies:

1. Kind of instruction:
   a. What special instruction shall be provided?
      1) Blind pupils?
      2) Deaf pupils?
      3) Crippled pupils?

4) Feeble-minded pupils?
5) Delinquent pupils?
6) Pupils failing in grades?
7) Backward or retarded pupils?
8) Incorrigible pupils?
9) Pupils permanently or temporarily confined in homes and hospitals because of illness or other causes of incapacity?

2. Appropriation:
   a. What shall be the annual appropriation for such special instruction?

Administrative Jobs

These and like administrative jobs should be delegated to the superintendent of schools:

1. Advise the school board as to appropriate instruction for the different types of handicapped pupils.
2. Provide such instruction for these pupils as the board of education may authorize.
3. Ascertain the annual appropriation required to carry on such instruction.
4. Keep adequate records on all matters pertaining to handicapped pupils and submit appropriate reports thereof to the board of education.

PROBLEM OR JOB: RELIGIOUS EDUCATION

Decisions made by a board of education on these and like issues are its policies:

1. Type:
   a. Shall public school pupils at the request of parents or guardians be dismissed for a period each week to go to the church of their choice for religious instruction?
   b. Shall a period be set aside in the public schools during which the different religious groups may be assigned rooms in which to give religious instruction to those pupils desiring it or whose parents desire them to have it?
2. Amount of time:
   a. How much school time shall be devoted weekly to such religious instruction?

3. Discipline and supervision:
   a. Who shall be responsible for the discipline and supervision of pupils while they are dismissed from the public schools for religious education?

Administrative Jobs

These and like administrative jobs should be delegated to the superintendent of schools:

1. Establish and maintain such facilities for religious education as the policies of the board require.
2. See to it that the necessary supervision is provided for pupils dismissed for religious instruction.
3. Prepare suitable reports on the problem of religious education and submit these to the school board.

―――

PROBLEM OR JOB: THRIFT EDUCATION

Decisions made by a board of education on these and like issues are its policies:

1. Establishment:
   a. Shall an educational thrift service be established in the public schools?
2. Legal obligations and responsibilities:
   a. What legal obligations and responsibilities do the school authorities assume in installing an educational thrift service?
3. Banks coöperating:
   a. What shall be the qualifications of banks asked to coöperate in public school educational thrift service?
4. Appropriation:
   a. What shall be the annual appropriation for thrift education and for educational thrift service?

Administrative Jobs

These and like administrative jobs should be delegated to the superintendent of schools:

1. Establish and operate such educational thrift service as the board may direct.
2. Ascertain the annual appropriation needed for conducting the thrift education program.

3. Keep adequate records of all matters pertaining to thrift education and make suitable reports thereof to the board of education.

PROBLEM OR JOB: SCHOOL GARDENS

Decisions made by a board of education on these and like issues are its policies:

1. Land:
   a. What land shall be secured and set aside for school gardens?
   b. Under what conditions may pupils secure plots for school gardens?
2. Seeds and equipment:
   a. What seeds and equipment shall be furnished pupils having school gardens?
   b. On what conditions?
3. Products:
   a. How shall products of school gardens be disposed of?
4. Income:
   a. How shall the income from school gardens be used?
5. Appropriations:
   a. What shall be the annual appropriation for school gardens?

Administrative Jobs

These and like administrative jobs should be delegated to the superintendent of schools:

1. Secure land for school gardens as policies of board require.
2. Lay out this land in plots and assign plots to pupils.
3. Provide the pupils such seeds and equipment as the policies of the board demand.
4. Supervise the work of pupils in the gardens.
5. Dispose of products of school gardens as the policies of the board require.
6. Place income from school gardens in such funds as the board of education may direct.
7. Ascertain the annual appropriation required for school gardens.
8. Keep adequate records of school gardens and submit appropriate reports thereof to the board of education.

PROBLEM OR JOB: PAGEANTS

Decisions made by a board of education on these and like issues are its policies:

1. Kind and number:
   a. What kind of pageants and how many may or shall the public schools sponsor during the year?
2. Participation:
   a. May other than public school pupils participate in these pageants?
3. Expenditures:
   a. What shall be the total annual expenditures for school pageants?
4. Appropriation:
   a. What shall be the annual appropriation for pageants?
5. Admission charges:
   a. What admission to pageants may be charged?
   b. How shall the income from admission charges for pageants be used?
6. Motion pictures:
   a. Under what conditions may the motion picture rights of pageants be sold?
   b. Shall the district have films of pageants made and kept as the property of the schools?
   c. What use may be made of such films?
   d. Under what conditions?

Administrative Jobs

These and like administrative jobs should be delegated to the superintendent of schools:

1. Prepare and present pageants.
2. Make the necessary expenditures for pageants.
3. Collect admission charges to pageants.
4. Sell motion picture rights to pageants.
5. Have films made of pageants.
6. Use these films as the policies of the board of education permit.
7. Ascertain the annual appropriation needed for pageants.
8. Keep the needed records on matters pertaining to pageants and submit suitable reports thereof to the school board.

PROBLEM OR JOB: BANDS AND ORCHESTRAS

Decisions made by a board of education on these and like issues are its policies:

1. Number and size:
   a. What bands and orchestras shall be sponsored in each division of the school system?
2. Equipment:
   a. Shall the school district furnish music, instruments, and uniforms for each member of bands and orchestras?
3. Membership:
   a. What shall be the requirements for membership in the respective bands and orchestras?
   b. May non-members of bands and orchestras appear in them on special occasions?
   c. If so, who and on what conditions?
4. Appearance at non-school functions:
   a. On what conditions may school bands and orchestras appear in non-school functions either at home or away from home?
5. Appropriations:
   a. What shall be the annual appropriation for orchestras and bands?

Administrative Jobs

These and like administrative jobs should be delegated to the superintendent of schools:

1. Organize and conduct bands and orchestras.
2. Purchase and distribute equipment for bands and orchestras as the policies of the board of education require.
3. Receive requests for bands and orchestras to play at non-school functions or activities.
4. Grant or deny such requests.
5. See that bands and orchestras are properly chaperoned when participating at non-school functions.
6. Ascertain the annual appropriation needed for bands and orchestras.
7. Keep adequate records of all matters pertaining to bands and orchestras and submit appropriate reports thereof to the board of education.

PROBLEM OR JOB: CLUBS AND OTHER ORGANIZATIONS

Decisions made by a board of education on these and like issues are its policies:

1. Kinds:
   a. Which of the following clubs may or shall be sponsored by the schools?
      1) Debating
      2) Garden
      3) Literary
      4) Rifle
      5) Student council
2. Membership:
   a. What shall be the qualifications for membership in each?
3. Supervision and coaching:
   a. What shall be the supervision and coaching provided for each club?
4. Equipment:
   a. Shall the district furnish rifles, etc., to members of the rifle club?
   b. Shall a rifle range for this club be purchased or rented?
5. Appropriations:
   a. What shall be the annual appropriation for these clubs?

Administrative Jobs

These and like administrative jobs should be delegated to the superintendent of schools:

1. Organize and supervise such clubs and other organizations as are in accord with the policies of the board.
2. Ascertain the annual appropriation required for such clubs and organizations.
3. Keep the needed records of such organizations and prepare appropriate reports thereof for the board of education.

PROBLEM OR JOB: ENTERTAINMENTS AND SOCIAL ACTIVITIES

Decisions made by a board of education on these and like issues are its policies:

1. Kind and number:

a. Which of the following entertainments and social activities may be sponsored by the public schools?
1) Carnivals
2) Circuses
3) Concerts
4) Dances
5) Moving picture shows
6) Parties
7) Picnics
8) Plays
9) Vaudeville

b. How many of each of these may be sponsored annually for or by each school group?

2. Regulation:
a. Who may attend or participate in each?
b. What admissions to each may be charged?
c. How shall each be supervised?
d. Where may each be held?
e. How shall receipts from each be used?
f. Who shall handle all funds connected with each?
g. What accounts shall be kept and what financial statements shall be made concerning each?
h. At what time of the day and week may each be held?
i. If held in the evening, at what hour must each close?
j. What shall constitute unbecoming conduct of pupils at these entertainments?
k. What shall be the penalty for such unbecoming conduct?

3. Appropriations:
a. What shall be the annual appropriation for each of these activities?

Administrative Jobs

These and like administrative jobs should be delegated to the superintendent of schools:

1. Provide and sponsor such entertainment and social activities as the policies of the board permit or require.
2. Enforce all rules and regulations pertaining to entertainments and social activities.
3. Ascertain the annual appropriation required for entertainments and social activities.

4. Keep adequate records of entertainments and social activities and submit appropriate reports thereof to the board of education.

Problem or Job: FRATERNITIES

Decisions made by a board of education on these and like issues are its policies:

1. Sanction or exclusion:
   a. Shall fraternities in the high school be sanctioned or excluded?
2. Substitutes:
   a. What substitutes for high school fraternities shall be provided?
   b. How shall such substitute organizations be promoted and fostered?
3. Violation of rule against fraternities:
   a. What shall be the penalty for violation of the rule prohibiting membership in a fraternity?

Administrative Jobs

This and like administrative jobs should be delegated to the superintendent of schools:

1. Enforce the rules and regulations of the board of education pertaining to fraternities.

Problem or Job: SOCIAL CENTERS

Decisions made by a board of education on these and like issues are its policies:

1. Kind and number:
   a. What community social centers shall the school district conduct alone or in coöperation with such non-school agencies as the Red Cross, Visiting Nurses Associations, or Parent-Teacher Associations?
2. Services:
   a. What services shall such social centers render?
3. Appropriations:
   a. What shall be the annual appropriation for community centers?

Administrative Jobs

These and like administrative jobs should be delegated to the superintendent of schools:

1. Organize and conduct social centers.
2. Have these social centers provide the activities for which they are organized.
3. Ascertain the annual appropriation needed for social centers.
4. Keep adequate records of such social centers and prepare appropriate reports thereof for the board of education.

PROBLEM OR JOB: PUBLIC LECTURES AND CONCERTS

Decisions made by a board of education on these and like issues are its policies:

1. Number and kind:
   a. What public lectures and concerts shall the public schools provide in the respective parts of the district each year?
   b. With what non-school agencies may or shall the schools coöperate in providing such public lectures and concerts?
2. Admission charges:
   a. What shall be the admission charges to these lectures and concerts?
3. Appropriations:
   a. What shall be the annual appropriation for public lectures and concerts?

Administrative Jobs

These and like administrative jobs should be delegated to the superintendent of schools:

1. Provide public lectures and concerts.
2. Coöperate with non-school agencies in promoting such lectures and concerts.
3. Collect admission charges to such lectures and concerts.
4. Ascertain the appropriations needed annually to conduct public lectures and concerts.
5. Keep adequate records of such lectures and concerts and prepare appropriate reports thereof for the board of education.

PROBLEM OR JOB: SCHOOL MUSEUMS

Decisions made by a board of education on these and like issues are its policies:

1. Space:
   a. What space shall be provided for school museums?
2. Specimens:
   a. How shall specimens for museums be secured?
   (See Gifts to Schools, page 139.)
3. Appropriations:
   a. What shall be the annual appropriation for school museums?

Administrative Jobs

These and like administrative jobs should be delegated to the superintendent of schools:

1. Provide space for school museums.
2. Secure appropriate specimens for school museums.
3. Prepare desirable rules and regulations for the use of such museums.
4. Ascertain the annual appropriation needed for school museums.
5. Keep adequate records of all matters pertaining to school museums and submit appropriate reports thereof to the board of education.

PROBLEM OR JOB: SCHOOL EXHIBITS

Decisions made by a board of education on these and like issues are its policies:

1. Kind and number:
   a. What exhibits of school work, and how many may or shall be prepared each year?
2. Appropriations:
   a. What shall be the annual appropriation for school exhibits?

Administrative Jobs

These and like administrative jobs should be delegated to the superintendent of schools:

1. Advise the board of education as to desirable school exhibits.

2. Determine the appropriation needed for such exhibits.
3. Prepare the exhibits.
4. Arrange for the public to view exhibits.
5. Keep adequate records on all matters pertaining to exhibits and prepare suitable reports thereon for the board of education.

_____

Problem or Job: SCHOLARSHIPS

Decisions made by a board of education on these and like issues are its policies:
1. Provided by district:
   a. What scholarships shall the district provide annually?
2. Other scholarships:
   a. See Gifts to Schools, page 139.
3. Basis of awarding:
   a. What shall be the qualifications of pupils to whom scholarships are awarded?
4. Appropriations:
   a. What shall be the annual appropriations for scholarships?

Administrative Jobs

These and like administrative jobs should be delegated to the superintendent of schools:
1. Secure funds for scholarships as the school board may direct.
2. Recommend to the board of education the use that the district should make of scholarships.
3. Award scholarships.
4. Ascertain the annual appropriation needed for scholarships.
5. Keep adequate records on all matters pertaining to scholarships and prepare suitable reports thereof for the board of education.

_____

Problem or Job: TELEPHONE SERVICE

Decisions made by a board of education on these and like issues are its policies:
1. Provision of telephones:
   a. What telephone service shall be provided in the different buildings?

2. Use by pupils and employees:
   a. What use may pupils and employees make of the school telephones?
3. Appropriations:
   a. What shall be the annual appropriation for telephone service?

Administrative Jobs

These and like administrative jobs should be delegated to the superintendent of schools:

1. Ascertain the telephones needed.
2. Have such telephone service established as the policies of the board require.
3. See that pupils and employees use telephones in accordance with policies of the board.
4. Pay for telephones.
5. Determine the annual appropriation required for telephone service.
6. Keep adequate records of telephone service and submit appropriate reports thereof to the board of education.

PROBLEM OR JOB: RELATION OF PUBLIC SCHOOLS TO LOCAL NON-PUBLIC SCHOOLS

Decisions made by a board of education on these and like issues are its policies:

1. What shall be the relation of the public schools to local schools?
   a. Parochial schools?
   b. Private elementary schools?
   c. Private secondary schools?

Administrative Jobs

These and like administrative jobs should be delegated to the superintendent of schools:

1. Establish and maintain that relation with non-public schools as is in accordance with the policies of the board of education.
2. Inspect and make such reports of non-public schools as the law requires.

3. Ascertain how more desirable relations can be established with non-public schools and make recommendations thereon to the board of education.

PROBLEM OR JOB: CENSUS AND ATTENDANCE OF PUPILS

Decisions made by a board of education on these and like issues are its policies:

1. Annual appropriation:
    a. What shall be the annual appropriation for the census and attendance department?
2. Content of census:
    a. What persons shall be included in the census?
    b. What information concerning each person in it shall the census contain?
    c. Shall a permanent and continuing census system be maintained?
3. School attendance of persons in census:
    a. What persons included in census shall be enrolled and in daily attendance at public, private, or parochial schools?
    b. Shall the attendance officers enforce attendance of non-public school pupils?
    c. What persons of compulsory school age may be excused from school attendance? Under what conditions?
    d. May high school seniors be excused from school from time graduation requirements are satisfied until date of graduation?
    e. What pupils may be granted work certificates?
4. Census enumerators and attendance officers:
    a. What shall be the qualifications of census enumerators and attendance officers?
    b. What shall be the term and salary schedule of census enumerators and attendance officers?
    c. Shall the census enumerators also be the attendance officers?
    d. What transportation shall the school district furnish census enumerators and attendance officers for use in the discharge of their duties?
    e. Leave of absence.
    (See Janitorial Service p. 125.)

Administrative Jobs

These and like administrative jobs should be delegated to the superintendent of schools:

1. Enforce the compulsory school law.
2. Educate parents on the importance of keeping their children in school.
3. Prosecute parents and guardians for failure to keep their children and wards in school as required by law.
4. Have incorrigibles and uncontrollable, recurring truancy cases committed to reform schools, special classes, special schools, etc.
5. Issue work certificates.
6. See to it that labor conditions for pupils issued work certificates conform to requirements of the law.
7. Keep in continuation school, as required by law, pupils who are granted work certificates.
8. Select and employ census enumerators and attendance officers.
9. Apply the salary schedule to census enumerators and attendance officers.
10. Determine and formulate the duties and responsibilities of these employees.
11. See to it that these employees perform their duties and responsibilities.
12. Grant or refuse leave of absence to these employees.
13. Keep adequate records of the work of the census and attendance department.
14. Prepare and submit at appropriate intervals suitable reports of the work of this department to the board of education.

PROBLEM OR JOB: TRANSPORTATION OF PUPILS

Decisions made by a board of education on these and like issues are its policies:

1. Annual appropriation:
   a. What shall be the annual appropriation for pupil transportation?
2. To whom transportation shall be furnished:
   a. What pupils shall be furnished transportation?

      1) Pupils living beyond certain distances from school buildings?

      2) Blind children?

      3) Crippled children?

3. Kind of transportation:

   a. What kind of transportation shall be provided?

      1) Bus?

      2) Street car?

4. Ownership of busses:

   a. Shall the school district own or rent the transportation busses?

5. Uses of busses:

   a. Shall busses be used for purposes other than the regular daily transportation of pupils?

6. Bus drivers:

   a. What shall be the salary schedule of bus drivers?

   b. What bond shall be required of bus drivers?

   c. Shall the school district provide workingmen's compensation insurance for bus drivers? If so, how much?

7. Operation of busses:

   a. What rules and regulations shall govern the operation of busses?

8. Insurance against accident and death from operation of busses:

   a. Shall the school district insure against accident and death pupils who are being transported?

   b. Shall the school district insure against injury and death from accidents incurred in operating transportation busses, of persons not transported?

   c. For what amount shall the school district carry insurance for *a* and *b*, respectively?

Administrative Jobs

These and like administrative jobs should be delegated to the superintendent of schools:

1. Designate particular pupils to be transported.
2. Lay out transportation routes.
3. Make changes in transportation routes.
4. Determine time schedule of busses.
5. Contract for transportation of pupils.

6. Enforce such contracts.
7. Purchase and distribute car tickets to pupils.
8. Purchase busses.
9. Purchase licenses for busses.
10. Purchase equipment and supplies for busses.
11. Maintain and repair busses.
12. Rent busses.
13. Formulate rules and regulations for the operation of busses.
14. Select and employ drivers of busses.
15. Approve or reject bonds of bus drivers.
16. Discipline, suspend, or discharge bus drivers.
17. Place workingmen's compensation insurance for bus drivers.
18. Place such insurance of busses and their operation as the policies of the board require.
19. Pay premiums on such insurance.
20. Collect insurance due under these policies and see to it that it is paid to the proper persons.

PROBLEM OR JOB: ADMISSION, TUITION, SUSPENSION, AND EXPULSION OF NONRESIDENT PUPILS

Decisions made by a board of education on these and like issues are its policies:
1. Schools to which they may be admitted:
    a. Shall nonresident pupils be admitted to
        1) Kindergartens?
        2) Elementary schools?
        3) Junior high schools?
        4) Senior high schools?
        5) Junior college?
        6) School of education?
        7) Evening schools?
        8) Continuation schools?
        9) Summer schools?
        10) Special schools for
            a.) Subnormal children?
            b.) Blind children?
            c.) Deaf children?

    d.) Crippled children?

    e.) Delinquent and incorrigible children?

2. Conditions on which they may be admitted:

    a. If they come from districts having educational offerings in these grades or for such pupils?

    b. If they come from districts not having educational offerings in these grades or for such pupils?

    c. If the state law requires it?

    d. If the buildings and equipment are strained in providing adequate facilities for resident pupils?

    e. If they come from outside the state and expect to live in the district temporarily?

3. Tuition:

    a. What shall determine tuition rates for the respective grades and schools:

        1) Cost?

        2) State law?

        3) Ability to pay?

    b. If a higher tuition rate is charged than the law requires the home district or county to pay, from whom shall the difference be collected?

    c. When shall tuition be paid?

    d. What shall be the penalty for nonpayment of tuition?

    e. What pupils shall be exempt from payment of part or all tuition?

    f. Under what conditions shall tuition be remitted?

    g. Into what fund shall the money collected for tuition be put?

4. Suspension or expulsion of nonresident pupils:

    a. Under what conditions shall nonresident pupils be suspended or expelled?

    b. Under what conditions shall a suspended or expelled nonresident pupil be readmitted?

Administrative Jobs

These and like administrative jobs should be delegated to the superintendent of schools:

1. Make contracts with proper authorities for admission of nonresident pupils.

2. Assign nonresident pupils to grades and buildings?

3. Keep adequate records of and make appropriate reports of attendance and progress of nonresident pupils.
4. Collect tuition.
5. Enforce penalty for nonpayment of tuition.
6. Grant or refuse requests for exemptions from payment of tuition.
7. Suspend and expel nonresident pupils.
8. Reinstate nonresident pupils who have been suspended or expelled.
9. Remit tuition.
10. Keep proper records and submit appropriate reports of the tuition collected and refunded.
11. Place collected tuition in appropriate fund.

PROBLEM OR JOB: SOLICITING SALES TO OR CONTRIBU-
TIONS FROM PUPILS

Decisions made by a board of education on these and like issues are its policies:

1. Soliciting to sell to pupils:

   a. May outside solicitors interview pupils at any time on school premises for the purpose of selling them magazines, books, etc.?

   b. May organizations, such as a Child Welfare Organization, sell tooth brushes, tooth powder, etc., to the children in school?

   c. Shall pupils be permitted to sell candy, etc., to pupils in schools in order to raise money for organizations such as Camp Fire Girls, Boy Scouts, athletic associations, etc.?

   d. May pupils sell tickets in school for lecture courses, student plays, etc., if the proceeds go for stadia, athletic prizes, making up deficits of school organizations or school activities, etc.?

   e. May pupils sell tickets in school for non-school plays and picture shows, if a portion of income from such play or picture show is given to school organizations or school activities?

   f. May subscriptions to school paper, high school annual, etc., be sought from pupils in schools?

2. Soliciting to secure contributions from pupils:
   a. May public school pupils be solicited in the schools to make contributions to such causes as
      1) Memorials?
      2) The relief of suffering resulting from such catastrophies as tornadoes, fires, earthquakes, etc.?
      3) School activities or gifts to schools?
3. Methods of soliciting pupils:
   a. May "Tag Day Campaigns" be conducted in the schools?
   b. May suitable boxes be placed in corridors so that pupils who desire may place contributions in these boxes?
   c. If so, how shall these boxes be supervised, and how shall their contents be handled?
   d. If such boxes are placed in corridors, what mention may be made of this to the pupils?

Administrative Jobs

These and like administrative jobs should be delegated to the superintendent of schools:
1. Admit or exclude outside solicitors.
2. Grant or refuse requests for placement of contribution boxes in corridors.
3. Supervise such boxes.
4. Transfer deposits from such boxes to the proper persons.
5. Grant or deny requests for permission to solicit sales or contributions in accordance with the policies of the board of education.
6. Supervise all soliciting.
7. Keep adequate records and make suitable reports to the board of education of all soliciting in the schools.

Problem or Job: DAMAGE OR LOSS OF PUPILS' PROPERTY IN SCHOOL

Decisions made by a board of education on these and like issues are its policies:
1. Responsibility:
   a. Shall the district be responsible for damage or loss of pupils' property in school?

2. Appropriation:
  a. If so, what shall be the annual appropriation to reimburse pupils for such damage or loss?

Administrative Jobs

These and like administrative jobs should be delegated to the superintendent of schools:

1. Reimburse pupils for damage to or loss of property, as the policies of the board require.
2. Ascertain the annual appropriation needed for reimbursement of pupils.
3. Keep adequate records of matters pertaining to damage or loss of pupils' property in school and submit appropriate reports thereof to the board of education.

———

PROBLEM OR JOB: DISCIPLINE IN SCHOOLS

Decisions made by a board of education on these and like issues are its policies:

1. Indolent pupils:
  a. What shall be done in the case of indolent pupils who waste their time and opportunity in school?
2. Incorrigible pupils:
  a. What classes, buildings, or special facilities shall be provided for incorrigible pupils?
  b. When shall incorrigible pupils be assigned to such classes or buildings?
  c. Under what conditions shall incorrigible pupils be turned over to the civil authorities?
3. Disobedience of groups of pupils:
  a. What shall be done in the case of groups of pupils who disobey or disregard the rules and regulations of the school?
4. Dress of pupils:
  a. Shall a uniform dress for high school pupils be adopted?
  b. If so, what shall be the penalty for violation of this standard of dress?
5. Suspension and expulsion of pupils:
  a. Under what conditions may or shall pupils be suspended or expelled?

6. Reinstatement of pupils:
   a. Under what conditions may or shall suspended or expelled pupils be reinstated?
7. Corporal punishment:
   a. When administered:
      1) Under what conditions may corporal punishment be administered to public school pupils?
   b. By whom administered:
      1) By whom shall such punishment be administered?
8. Trespass on and destruction and theft of property:
   a. How shall the school authorities proceed if either school or non-school property is broken, damaged, destroyed, or trespassed on by
      1) Pupils while schools are in session?
      2) Pupils while schools are not in session?
9. Law suits against school employees for disciplining pupils:
   a. What aid shall the school district render employees sued for enforcing discipline in schools?
10. Appropriations:
   a. What shall be the annual appropriation for disciplinary facilities?

Administrative Jobs

These and like administrative jobs should be delegated to the superintendent of schools:

1. Carry out the policies of the board with respect to indolent pupils.
2. Provide classes, buildings, etc., for incorrigible pupils.
3. Coöperate with juvenile court authorities in handling incorrigible pupils.
4. Enforce rules and regulations relating to dress of pupils.
5. Suspend, expel, and reinstate pupils.
6. Administer corporal punishment.
7. Carry out the policies of the board in cases of trespass on or destruction and theft of property by pupils while in school or on their way to or from school.
8. Enforce rules and regulations relating to pupils trespassing on property while at school or while on way to or from school.
9. Provide such assistance to employees being sued for disciplining pupils as the policies of the board require.

10. Ascertain the appropriation needed annually for disciplinary facilities.

11. Keep adequate records of all matters pertaining to discipline and submit appropriate reports thereon to the board of education.

————

PROBLEM OR JOB: ADMISSION OF PUPILS

Decisions made by a board of education on these and like issues are its policies:

1. Conditions of entrance:
    a. To enter the different divisions, grades, and courses, what requirements shall pupils satisfy with respect to:
        1) Residence
           (See Nonresident Pupils, page 54.)
        2) Age
        3) Health
        4) Training
    b. When during the school term may pupils be admitted to the respective divisions, courses, and grades?

Administrative Jobs

These and like administrative jobs should be delegated to the superintendent of schools:

1. Grant or refuse requests for pupils to enter school.
2. Keep adequate records of admission of pupils and submit appropriate reports thereon to the board of education.

————

PROBLEM OR JOB: CLASSIFICATION AND PROGRESS OF PUPILS

Decisions made by a board of education on these and like issues are its policies:

1. Basis of classification and promotion:
    a. In classifying and promoting pupils, what use shall be made of:
        1) Age?
        2) Sex?
        3) Race?

4) Health?
5) Intelligence quotient?
6) Accomplishment quotient?
7) Index of maturity?
8) Social index?
9) Length of time in school and grade?
10) Standard tests?
11) Teachers' marks?
12) School examinations?
13) Recommendations of guidance bureau?
2. Frequency of reclassification and promotion:
   a. At what intervals shall pupils be reclassified and promoted?

Administrative Jobs

These and like administrative jobs should be delegated to the superintendent of schools:

1. Classify and promote pupils.
2. Keep adequate records of the classification and progress of pupils and submit appropriate reports thereon to the board of education.

———

Problem or Job: TRANSFER OF PUPILS

Decisions made by a board of education on these and like issues are its policies:

1. Basis of transfer:
   a. On what conditions may or shall pupils transfer
   1) From one building to another?
   2) From one teacher to another?
   3) From one course to another?
   4) From one department to another?

Administrative Jobs

These and like administrative jobs should be delegated to the superintendent of schools:

1. Receive requests for transfer of pupils.
2. Grant or deny such requests.
3. Transfer pupils as the policies of the board require.
4. Keep adequate records of transfer of pupils and submit appropriate reports thereon to the board of education.

PROBLEM OR JOB: GRADUATION OF PUPILS

Decisions made by a board of education on these and like issues are its policies:

1. Requirements:
    a. For graduation from the respective divisions and courses of study, what requirements shall pupils satisfy with respect to:
        1) Attendance in residence?
        2) Subjects pursued?
        3) Age?
        4) Grades on
            a) Standard tests?
            b) School examinations?
        5) Teachers' marks?
2. Date of certification:
    a. What shall be the final date for certification of pupils for graduation?
3. Invitations and announcements:
    a. By whom shall invitations and announcements be supplied?
    b. What amount shall be appropriated for invitations and announcements?
4. Salutatorian and valedictorian:
    a. What shall be the respective qualifications of the salutatorian and the valedictorian?
5. Dress, flowers, and gifts:
    a. Shall there be a regulation governing dress, flowers, and gifts of graduates at commencement exercises?
6. Graduation exercises:
    a. What shall be the annual appropriation for graduation exercises?
    b. What shall be the qualifications of the commencement speaker and of the minister delivering the baccalaureate sermon?
    c. Shall the commencement speaker and minister for the baccalaureate sermon selected by the superintendent be approved?
7. Diplomas and certificates of graduation:
    a. What shall be the annual appropriation for diplomas and certificates of graduation?

Administration Jobs

These and like administrative jobs should be delegated to the superintendent of schools.

1. See to it that candidates for graduation have satisfied all requirements.
2. Certify pupils for graduation.
3. Have graduation invitations and announcements furnished in accordance with the policies of the board.
4. Select the valedictorian and the salutatorian.
5. Enforce all rules and regulations relating to dress, flowers, and gifts of graduates at commencement exercises.
6. Select the speaker for the commencement address and the minister for the baccalaureate sermon.
7. Purchase diplomas and certificates of graduation.
8. Present diplomas and certificates of graduation.
9. Ascertain the appropriation needed for graduation exercises each year.
10. Keep adequate records of graduation of pupils and submit appropriate reports thereon to the board of education.

―――

PROBLEM OR JOB: INJURY AND DEATH OF PERSONS ON SCHOOL PREMISES

Decisions made by a board of education on these and like issues are its policies:

1. Action to be taken:
   a. What shall be done in cases of injury and death of pupils, employees, or visitors incurred:
      1) On school playgrounds?
      2) On athletic fields and in gymnasiums? (See Accidents in Athletics, page 31).
      3) In shops and laboratories?
      4) On stairways and in corridors?
      5) In classrooms and auditoriums?
      6) In transportation busses? (See Transportation of Pupils, page 52).
   b. Shall the accidents occurring during school hours be handled differently from those occurring outside of school hours?

2. Type of insurance:
   a. Shall the district insure all persons against injuries and death occurring in situations listed under 1 above?
   b. What shall be the qualifications of companies furnishing such insurance?
3. Appropriation:
   a. What shall be the annual appropriation for handling such cases of injury and death?

Administrative Jobs

These and like administrative jobs should be delegated to the superintendent of schools:

1. Carry out the policies of the board of education with respect to accidents occurring to persons on public school premises.
2. Purchase insurance to cover injuries and accidents incurred on school property.
3. Pay premiums on such insurance.
4. Collect insurance in cases of accidents and see that it is paid to the proper persons.
5. Ascertain the annual appropriation needed for handling such accidents.
6. Keep adequate records of all matters pertaining to injury and death of persons on school premises and submit appropriate reports thereon to the board of education.

PROBLEM OR JOB: PROTECTION OF PUPILS IN CITY TRAFFIC

Decisions made by a board of education on these and like issues are its policies:

1. Inadequate traffic protection:
   a. In case the city provides inadequate traffic protection to the public school pupils, what action shall the district take?
2. Safety signs:
   a. In case the city provides inadequate safety signs near public school buildings what action shall the district take?

Administrative Jobs

These and like administrative jobs should be delegated to the superintendent of schools:

1. Ascertain the adequacy of traffic protection furnished public school pupils.
2. Make recommendations to the board of education as to what action should be taken to secure greater traffic protection for the pupils and more safety signs near the public school buildings.
3. Make the necessary arrangements with the city government for such traffic protection and safety signs as are needed.

PROBLEM OR JOB: REPORTS TO PARENTS

Decisions made by a board of education on these and like issues are its policies:

1. Kind and frequency:
   a. What reports shall be made to parents of pupils?
   b. At what intervals shall such reports be made?

Administrative Jobs

This and like administrative jobs should be delegated to the superintendent of schools:

1. Make suitable reports to parents on attendance and progress of children in schools.

PROBLEM OR JOB: TRANSPORTATION, TUITION, AND LODGING FOR PUPILS ATTENDING OTHER SCHOOLS

Decisions made by a board of education on these and like issues are its policies:

1. When furnished:
   a. Under what conditions shall the district pay tuition, transportation, and lodging for pupils attending other than the local district schools?
2. Appropriations:
   a. What shall be the annual appropriation for tuition, transportation, and lodging of pupils attending other than the local district schools?

Administrative Jobs

These and like administrative jobs should be delegated to the superintendent of schools:

1. Receive requests for payment of tuition, transportation, and lodging for pupils desiring to attend other than local district schools.
2. Grant or deny such requests.
3. Ascertain the annual appropriation needed for tuition, transportation, and lodging of pupils attending other than local district schools.
4. Keep adequate records of tuition, transportation, and lodging for pupils attending other than local district schools and submit appropriate reports thereof to the board of education.

PROBLEM OR JOB: THE ORGANIZATION OF THE PUBLIC SCHOOLS

Decisions made by a board of education on these and like issues are its policies:

1. Divisions of the public school organization:
    a. Into what divisions (Education, Business, Research, etc.,) shall the work of the public schools be divided?
2. Internal organization of each division:
    a. What shall be the internal organization of each division?
3. Work of each division:
    a. What shall be the work of each division and of each subdivision?
4. Relation of divisions to one another:
    a. What shall be the relation of the respective divisions and subdivisions to one another?

Administrative Jobs

These and like administrative jobs should be delegated to the superintendent of schools:

1. Advise the board of education as to the most desirable organization of the public schools.
2. Organize the public schools as policies of the board require.
3. Assign the work of each division.
4. See that each division does the work assigned it.

5. See that the proper relations are maintained within the school organization.

Problem or Job: ORGANIZATION OF EDUCATIONAL DIVISION

Decisions made by a board of education on these and like issues are its policies:

1. Departments:
   a. Into what departments shall the work of the educational division be divided:
      1) Kindergartens?
      2) Elementary schools?
      3) Junior high schools?
      4) Senior high schools?
      5) Junior colleges?
      6) Continuation schools?
      7) Evening schools?
      8) Special vocational schools?
      9) Summer schools?
      10) Experimental schools?
      11) Extension division?

Administrative Jobs

These and like administrative jobs should be delegated to the superintendent of schools:

1. Advise the school board as to the desirable organization of the Educational Division.
2. Organize the work of the Educational Division into the schools and departments authorized by the board.

Problem or Job: INTERNAL ORGANIZATION OF EDUCATIONAL DIVISION

Decisions made by a board of education on these and like issues are its policies:

1. What it shall be:
   a. On which of the following plans shall the respective schools be organized:

    1) Usual or conventional plan?
    2) Platoon system?
    3) Dalton plan?
    4) Winnetka plan?

Administrative Jobs

These and like administrative jobs should be delegated to the superintendent of schools:

1. Advise the board of education as to the desirable internal organization of the Educational Division.
2. Establish and maintain such internal organization of the Educational Division as the policies of the board require.

Problem or Job: ORGANIZATION OF BUSINESS DIVISION

Decisions made by a board of education on these and like issues are its policies:

1. Departments:
    a. Into what departments shall the work of the Business Division be divided?
        1) Buildings and grounds?
        2) Maintenance and operation of school plant?
        3) Purchasing?
        4) Financial accounting?
        5) Legal?

Administrative Jobs

These and like administrative jobs should be delegated to the superintendent of schools:

1. Advise the board of education as to the desirable form of organization of the Business Division.
2. Organize the Business Division as the policies of the board of education require.

Problem or Job: ORGANIZATION AND WORK OF RESEARCH DIVISION

Decisions made by a board of education on these and like issues are its policies:

1. Departments:
    a. Into what departments shall the work of the Research Division be divided:
        1) Educational research?
        2) Business research?
2. Work of:
    a. What shall be the work of each department of the Research Division?
3. Appropriation:
    a. What shall be the annual appropriation for the respective departments of the Research Division?

Administrative Jobs

These and like administrative jobs should be delegated to the superintendent of schools:

1. Advise the school board as to the organization and work of the Research Division.
2. Organize the Research Division as the policies of the board of education require.
3. Assign the work of the Research Division.
4. See that the Research Division does the work assigned it.
5. Ascertain the annual appropriation needed for the respective departments of the Research Division.
6. Keep adequate records of all matters pertaining to the organization and work of the Research Division and submit appropriate reports thereon to the board of education.

PROBLEM OR JOB: THE SCHOOL CALENDAR

Decisions made by a board of education on these and like issues are its policies:

1. Content:
    a. Date of opening of schools.
    b. Date of closing of schools.
    c. Dates of holidays and vacations.
    d. Date for members of the instructional staff to report for duty.
2. The school term:
    a. Divisions:
        1) Into what divisions shall the school term be divided?

2) How long shall each division of the school term be?
3) What shall be the date of opening and closing of each division of the school term?

3. Closing of schools:
   a. Purpose of:
      1) For which of the following reasons shall the schools be closed?
         a) Teachers' meetings?
         b) Storms?
         c) Epidemics?
         d) Holidays and vacations:
            (1) Columbus Day?
            (2) Armistice Day?
            (3) Thanksgiving Day?
            (4) Christmas?
            (5) Washington's Birthday?
            (6) Lincoln's Birthday?
            (7) Easter?
         e) Death of members of instructional staff?
         f) Special occasions?
   b. For how long:
      1) How long shall the schools be closed for each of the above reasons?
      2) Shall days of the term lost by closing the schools for each of the above reasons be made up?

4. Changes in calendar:
   a. Under what conditions shall changes be made in the school calendar?

5. Date of adoption:
   a. On what date shall the school calendar be adopted?
   b. Shall the calendar prepared by the superintendent be adopted?

Administrative Jobs

These and like administrative jobs should be delegated to the superintendent of schools:

1. Prepare the calendar and submit it to the board of education for approval and adoption.
2. Open and close the schools in accordance with the calendar adopted by the school board.

3. Recommend changes in the calendar.
4. Make such changes in the calendar as the board of education authorizes.
5. Have the schools make up such days as the policies of the school board require.
6. Keep adequate records of all matters pertaining to the school calendar.
7. Submit appropriate reports thereof to the board of education.

———

PROBLEM OR JOB: THE SCHOOL DAY

Decisions made by a board of education on these and like issues are its policies:

1. Length:
   a. What shall be the length of the school day for the respective grades and divisions?
2. Hours of opening and closing:
   a. At what time shall the school day open and close in the different grades and divisions?
3. Intermissions:
   a. What intermissions shall be observed in each grade each day?
   b. What shall be the purpose of intermissions?
4. Time and length of intermissions:
   a. What shall be the length of the different intermissions in the respective grades and divisions?
   b. At what hour shall each intermission in the different grades and divisions come?

Administrative Jobs

These and like administrative jobs should be delegated to the superintendent of schools:

1. Advise the board of education on all matters relating to:
   a. The length of the school day.
   b. The hour of opening and closing sessions.
   c. The time and length of intermissions.
2. See that the school day is carried out as the policies of the school board require.

PROBLEM OR JOB: PROGRAMS AND EXERCISES FOR
SPECIAL DAYS

Decisions made by a board of education on these and like issues are its policies:

1. Designation of special days:
   a. Which of the following shall be designated as days on which special programs or exercises shall be held in the public schools:
      1) Roosevelt Day?
      2) Columbus Day?
      3) Memorial Day?
      4) Woodrow Wilson Day?
      5) Washington's Birthday?
      6) Lincoln's Birthday?
      7) Vegetable Days?
      8) Thrift Days?
      9) Good English Days?
   b. What special programs or exercises shall be held on each of these days?
2. Appropriations:
   a. What shall be the annual appropriation for programs and exercises for special days?

Administrative Jobs

These and like administrative jobs should be delegated to the superintendent of schools:

1. Advise the board of education as to the programs and exercises that shall be held in the public schools:
   a. Armstice Day.
   b. Thanksgiving Day.
   c. Health Day.
   d. Arbor Day.
2. Prepare and present such programs and exercises as the policies of the board require.
3. Ascertain the annual appropriation needed for programs and exercises for special days.
4. Keep adequate records of all matters pertaining to programs and exercises for special days and submit appropriate reports thereof to the board of education.

PROBLEM OR JOB: THE WORK OF MEMBERS OF THE INSTRUCTIONAL STAFF

Decisions made by a board of education on these and like issues are its policies:

1. Duties and responsibilities:
   a. What shall be the duties and responsibilities of each type of position held by members of the instructional staff?
   b. What clerical work shall members of the instructional staff be expected to perform outside of regular duties?
2. Length of day:
   a. How many hours per day or week shall members of the instructional staff be expected to give to their regular work?
3. Teaching load:
   a. What number of classes in the respective courses and subjects shall constitute a teacher's load?
   b. What shall be the minimum and maximum size of class in the respective courses, subjects, and grades?

Administrative Jobs

These and like administrative jobs should be delegated to the superintendent of schools:

1. Advise the school board on all matters pertaining to the work of the instructional staff.
2. Assign duties and responsibilities to each member of the instructional staff.
3. Reassign the duties and responsibilities of members of the instructional staff.
4. See to it that the respective members of the instructional staff do the work assigned them.
5. Ascertain that each member of the instructional staff is assigned a standard load.

PROBLEM OR JOB: QUALIFICATIONS AND THE SELECTION AND EMPLOYMENT OF MEMBERS OF THE INSTRUCTIONAL STAFF

Decisions made by a board of education on these and like issues are its policies:

1. Qualifications:

a. In the respective divisions and departments of the school system, what shall be the qualifications of new entrants in the position of:

1) Assistant superintendent
2) Principal
3) Supervisor
4) Special teacher
5) Head of department
6) Regular teacher
7) Coach
8) Part-time teacher
9) Military instructor
10) Substitute teacher
11) Assistant

with respect to:

1) Age?
2) Health?
3) Citizenship?
4) Patriotism?
5) Nationality?
6) Race?
7) Residence?
8) Church affiliation?
9) Marriage?
10) Academic training?
11) Professional training?
12) Teaching experience?
13) Supervisory experience?
14) Administrative experience?
15) Certification?

b. In the case of reappointments to such positions, what shall be the qualifications?

2. Selection and employment:

a. Shall the persons nominated by the superintendent of schools for positions on the instructional staff be approved?

b. In the selection and employment of members of the instructional staff, shall such classifications as assigned list, probationary period, and permanent tenure be defined and used?

Administrative Jobs

These and like administrative jobs should be delegated to the superintendent of schools:

1. Advise the board of education as to the qualifications desirable or needed in the respective positions on the instructional staff.
2. Advise the school board as to the desirability of such classifications as assigned list, probationary period, and permanent tenure.
3. Make nominations for the respective positions on the instructional staff.
4. Employ such persons for positions on the instructional staff as the board of education approves.
5. Execute contracts with persons elected to positions on the instructional staff.
6. Keep adequate records of all matters pertaining to the selection and employment of members of the instructional staff and submit appropriate reports thereof to the board of education.

PROBLEM OR JOB: CONTRACTS WITH MEMBERS OF THE INSTRUCTIONAL STAFF

Decisions made by a board of education on these and like issues are its policies:

1. Form and content:
   a. What shall be the form and content of contracts with members of the instructional staff?
2. Signature and return:
   a. Within what period of time after the election of a member of the instructional staff shall he be required to sign and return the contract?
   b. What shall be the penalty for failure to sign and return the contract within this time?
3. Violation:
   a. What action shall be taken in the case of a member of the instructional staff who violates his contract?
   b. Shall the State Department of Education be notified of such violation?

4. Release:
  a. Shall a member of the instructional staff be released from the contract in order:
    1) That he may accept a like position in another school system?
    2) That he may accept a different position in another school system?
    3) That he may go into another vocation?
    4) That (in the case of a woman teacher) she may marry?
  b. Shall a member of the instructional staff be released from the contract on account of illness?
    1) Of himself?
    2) Of a member of his family?
  c. Conditions of release:
    1) How long in advance of the date when the release is to go into effect must the request for it be in the hands of the superintendent?
5. Revocation:
  a. Under what conditions shall contracts with members of the instructional staff be revoked?

Administrative Jobs

These and like administrative jobs should be delegated to the superintendent of schools:

1. Advise the school board on all matters relating to contracts with members of the instructional staff.
2. Execute all contracts with the members of the instructional staff.
3. Enforce such penalties for violation of contracts by members of the instructional staff as the policies of the board require.
4. Receive requests for release of members of instructional staff from contracts.
5. Grant or refuse such requests.
6. Revoke contracts for causes designated by the board of education.
7. Keep adequate records on all matters pertaining to contracts with members of the instructional staff and submit appropriate reports thereof to the board of education.

PROBLEM OR JOB: ORGANIZATION OF THE INSTRUC-
TIONAL STAFF

Decisions made by a board of education on this and like
issues are its policies:

1. Divisions and departments:
   a. How shall the instructional staff of each school building
   be organized?

Administrative Jobs

These and like administrative jobs should be delegated to the
superintendent of schools:

1. Advise the school board as to how the instructional staff
   of each school building should be organized.
2. Organize the work of the instructional staff in accordance
   with the policies of the board of education.

PROBLEM OR JOB: ASSIGNMENT AND TRANSFER OF
MEMBERS OF INSTRUCTIONAL STAFF

Decisions made by a board of education on these and like
issues are its policies:

1. Assignment:
   a. Shall members of the instructional staff be employed for
   specific positions?
2. Transfer:
   a. Under what conditions shall members of the instructional staff be transferred:
      1) From one building to another?
      2) From one grade to another?
      3) From one subject to another?
      4) From one department to another?

Administrative Jobs

These and like administrative jobs should be delegated to the
superintendent of schools:

1. Advise the board of education on all matters pertaining to
   the assignment and transfer of members of the instructional
   staff.
2. Assign and transfer members of the instructional staff.

3. Keep adequate records of all matters pertaining to assignment and transfer of members of instructional staff and submit appropriate reports thereon to the board of education.

PROBLEM OR JOB: LEAVE OF ABSENCE FOR MEMBERS OF INSTRUCTIONAL STAFF

Decisions made by a board of education on these and like issues are its policies:

1. Shall a member of the instructional staff be granted leave of absence.
    a. On account of illness:
        1) Of himself?
        2) Of a member of his immediate family?
        3) Of a distant relative?
        4) Of a friend?
    b. On account of the death:
        1) Of a member of his immediate family?
        2) Of a distant relative?
        3) Of a friend?
    c. On account of contagious disease in the home in which he lives?
    d. For rest?
    e. For travel?
    f. For study?
    g. For visiting schools?
    h. For attendance of educational meetings:
        1) National?
        2) State?
        3) District?
        4) County?
        5) Local?
    i. For attendance of non-educational meetings:
        1) Rotarian?
        2) Kiwanis?
        3) Chamber of Commerce?
    j. For service in the National Guards?
    k. For service in Reserve Officers Training Camps?
2. In each of the preceding cases:
    a. Under what conditions may a member of the instructional

staff conclude his work before the close of the day or the close of the term?

b. For how long a period may a member of the instructional staff be granted leave of absence?

c. Under what conditions may a leave of absence be extended?

d. At what intervals may leaves of absence be granted to the same person?

e. What part of an individual's salary shall be paid him while he is on leave of absence?

f. Shall any of the expenses incurred by a person on leave of absence be paid by the district?

g. What shall be the penalty for failure to report for duty immediately upon the expiration of a leave?

h. What shall be the penalty for using a leave of absence for a different purpose than that for which it is granted?

i. Under what conditions shall a leave of absence be cancelled?

Administrative Jobs

These and like administrative jobs should be delegated to the superintendent of schools:

1. Grant or refuse requests for leave of absence.
2. Pay that part of an individual's salary due him while on leave of absence.
3. Pay such expenses incurred by persons on leave as the policies of the board of education require.
4. Enforce the penalties for failure to comply with all the rules of the board of education pertaining to leaves of absence.
5. Keep a proper and complete record of all leaves of absence.
6. Submit appropriate reports on leaves of absence to the board of education.

PROBLEM OR JOB: IMPROVEMENT OF THE MEMBERS OF INSTRUCTIONAL STAFF WHILE IN SERVICE

Decisions made by a board of education on these and like issues are its policies:

1. Annual appropriations:

    a. What shall be the annual appropriation for the improvement, while in service, of teachers, supervisors, and principals, respectively?

    b. What shall be the annual appropriation for each means of improvement used?

2. Means:

    a. Which of the following means shall be employed in the improvement of teachers, supervisors, and principals while in service:

        1) Consultative service from outside experts?

        2) Instruction by better-trained members of the staff?

        3) Extension courses and lectures from higher educational institutions?

        4) Correspondence courses from higher educational institutions?

        5) Summer schools in higher educational institutions?

        6) Leave of absence (sabbatical leave) for semester or year for study or for travel?

        7) Change to part-time work basis so as to study part time in an approved institution?

        8) Exchange positions for a semester or a year with members of corresponding rank in instructional staff of another city?

        9) Professional meetings for members of the staff?

        10) Attendance at and participation in conventions held by local, county, district, state, and national professional organizations?

        11) Visitation of other teachers at work?

        12) Visitation of other schools within the system?

        13) Visitation of schools outside of the system?

3. Extent:

    a. To what extent shall the individual members of the instructional staff avail themselves of each of the foregoing means of improvement?

    b. What shall be the penalty for failure to seek improvement by some of the above means?

    c. What shall be the reward for making use of the respective means of improvement while in service?

4. Cost:

    a. What part of the cost of each means of improvement

shall be borne by the individual member of the staff profiting from it?

   b. What use shall be made of:

      1) Scholarship funds?

      2) Teacher loan funds?

5. Salary increases:

   a. What more than mere attendance at meetings or courses shall constitute the additional training which will enable a member of the instructional staff to pass to a higher rating on the salary schedule?

   b. When, after the individual has completed the required additional training, shall his salary be adjusted to conform with the salary schedule?

Administrative Jobs

These and like administrative jobs should be delegated to the superintendent of schools:

1. Advise the board of education on the means that should be employed for the improvement of teachers, supervisors, and principals in service.

2. See that members of the instructional staff avail themselves of such means of improvement while in service as the policies of the board require.

3. Enforce penalties for failure of members of the instructional staff to make use of such means of improvement as the board policies require.

4. Give recognition and pay rewards for making use of means of improvement in accordance with policies of the board of education.

5. Ascertain the annual appropriation needed for carrying on the work of improvement of the instructional staff in service.

6. Make arrangements for such scholarship funds and teacher loan funds as the policies of the board of education demand.

7. Administer such scholarship and loan funds.

8. Keep adequate records of all matters pertaining to the improvement of members of the instructional staff while in service and submit appropriate reports thereof to the board of education.

PROBLEM OR JOB: ATTENDANCE OF EMPLOYEES AT PROFESSIONAL MEETINGS AND CONVENTIONS

Decisions made by a board of education on these and like issues are its policies:

1. Appropriations:
   a. What annual appropriation shall be made to pay employees' expenses to professional meetings and conventions?
   b. What shall be the annual appropriation for substitutes who fill the positions of members of the regular staff while these are in attendance at professional meetings and conventions?
2. Number of employees to attend conventions:
   a. How many employees may or shall attend each of the educational conventions held during the year?
3. Obligations of employees who attend conventions:
   a. What obligations or responsibilities shall each employee assume who secures leave of absence to attend or who is designated by the superintendent to attend an educational meeting?
   b. If the schools are closed in order that the teachers may attend conventions, what shall be done in the case of teachers who, instead of attending all or part of the sessions.
      1) Stay at home?
      2) Visit other cities or go camping?
      3) Spend their time shopping, attending theater?
4. Closing schools for professional conventions:
   a. Shall the schools be closed in order that teachers may attend educational meetings and conventions?
   b. If so, for how many days during the term?
5. Part of each employee's expense which district shall bear:
   a. What part of an employee's expense incurred in attending a professional meeting shall the district pay?

Administrative Jobs

These and like administrative jobs should be delegated to the superintendent of schools:

1. Advise the board of education as to the number of employees that should attend educational conventions during the year.

2. Select the employees that are to attend such conventions at the expense of the district.
3. Advise the school board as to the desirability of closing schools for the different educational meetings and conventions.
4. See to it that employees securing leave of absence to attend educational meetings and conventions perform such obligations and responsibilities connected therewith as the policies of the board require.
5. Enforce the penalties that the policies of the board stipulate for failure of employees to fulfill such obligations and responsibilities.
6. Close the schools as the policies of the board demand for educational meetings and conventions.
7. Pay such part of employees' expenses incurred in attending educational meetings and conventions as the policies of the board demand.
8. Ascertain the annual appropriation needed to carry out the policies of the board with respect to attendance of employees at educational meetings and conventions.
9. Keep adequate records of attendance of employees at professional meetings and conventions and submit appropriate reports thereof to the board of education.

PROBLEM OR JOB: SALARY SCHEDULE OF INSTRUCTIONAL STAFF

Decisions made by a board of education on these and like issues are its policies:

1. Salaries of respective positions:
    a. Shall the salaries of members of the instructional staff in similar positions be the same irrespective of sex, provided that training and experience has been the same?
    b. Shall the salaries of members of the instructional staff be the same irrespective of the grade of pupils taught, provided that training and experience has been the same?
    c. What shall be the salaries of the respective positions occupied by members of the instructional staff?
    d. Under what conditions shall arrangements not in accordance with the salary schedule be made?

    e. Shall the members of the instructional staff be paid on a 9- , 10- , or 12-month basis?

2. Salary increases:

    a. Upon what basis shall salary increases be made?

    b. What shall be sufficient evidence that a member has completed the additional training necessary to place him on a higher rating of the salary schedule?

    c. When, after a member of the instructional staff has satisfied the requirements for an increase of salary shall such salary increase go into effect?

3. The bonus:

    a. What use shall be made of the bonus in connection with the payment of members of the instructional staff?

4. Salary deductions:

    a. Shall the salaries of members of the instructional staff go on

        1) While the schools are closed by order of the board of health because of an epidemic?

        2) While the schools are closed by order of the board of education because of an epidemic?

        3) While the schools are closed because of a shortage of fuel?

        4) While the schools are closed for vacations and holidays?

    b. Shall members of the instructional staff have their salaries docked because of tardiness or absence due to

        1) Avoidable causes?

        2) Unavoidable causes?

5. Appropriations:

    a. What shall be the annual appropriation for salaries of the instructional staff?

Administrative Jobs

These and like administrative jobs should be delegated to the superintendent of schools:

1. Advise the board of education as to the principles that should govern in the making of a salary schedule.

2. Apply the salary schedule to the respective positions and jobs in the school system.

3. Grant and deny requests for salary increases.

4. Make salary deductions as the board's policies require.

5. Pay such bonuses as are provided for by the policies of the board.
6. Ascertain the annual appropriation needed for salaries of the instructional staff.
7. Keep adequate records of all matters pertaining to salary schedule of instructional staff and submit appropriate report thereof to the board of education.

———

PROBLEM OR JOB: TRANSPORTATION OF MEMBERS OF INSTRUCTIONAL STAFF

Decisions made by a board of education on these and like issues are its policies:
1. To whom:
   a. What members of the instructional staff shall be provided transportation?
   b. Under what conditions shall transportation be furnished such members of the instructional staff?
2. Kind:
   a. What transportation facilities shall be provided such members of the instructional staff?
3. Appropriation:
   a. What shall be the annual appropriation for such transportation?

Administrative Jobs

These and like administrative jobs should be delegated to the superintendent of schools:
1. Advise the board of education as to the transportation that should be provided the respective members of the instructional staff.
2. Provide such transportation for the members of the instructional staff as the policies of the board of education require.
3. Ascertain the annual appropriation needed for transportation of members of the instructional staff.
4. Keep adequate records of all matters pertaining to the transportation of the members of the instructional staff and submit appropriate reports thereof to the board of education.

PROBLEM OR JOB: PENSIONS AND RETIREMENT FUNDS FOR MEMBERS OF INSTRUCTIONAL STAFF

Decisions made by a board of education on these and like issues are its policies:

1. Establishment and maintenance:
   a. Shall pensions and retirement funds for members of the instructional staff be established and maintained?
2. Sources of income:
   a. From what sources shall incomes for such pension and retirement funds be secured?
3. Appropriations:
   a. What shall be the annual appropriation for such pension and retirement funds?

Administrative Jobs

These and like administrative jobs should be delegated to the superintendent of schools:

1. Advise the board of education on the establishment and operation of pension and retirement funds.
2. Administer such funds.
3. Ascertain the annual appropriation needed for pension and retirement funds.
4. Keep adequate records on all matters pertaining to pensions and retirement funds for members of instructional staff and submit appropriate reports thereof to the board of education.

PROBLEM OR JOB: TEACHERS' ORGANIZATIONS

Decisions made by a board of education on these and like issues are its policies:

1. Membership:
   a. In what teachers' organizations may membership be held by members of the instructional staff?
2. Activities:
   a. What activities of teachers' organizations shall be approved?
3. Penalty for violation of board rules and regulations:
   a. What shall be the penalty for violation of rules and regulations in regard to membership in teachers' organization?

Administrative Jobs

These and like administrative jobs should be delegated to the superintendent of schools:

1. Advise the board of education on matters relating to teachers' organizations.
2. Enforce the rules and regulations of the board as these apply to membership in teachers' organizations.
3. Keep adequate records of all matters pertaining to teachers' organizations and submit appropriate reports thereof to the board of education.

PROBLEM OR JOB: SUSPENSION, RESIGNATION, RETIREMENT, AND REINSTATEMENT OF MEMBERS OF THE INSTRUCTIONAL STAFF

Decisions made by a board of education on these and like issues are its policies:

1. Condition:
   a. Under what conditions may or shall members of the instructional staff be
      1) Suspended?
      2) Retired?
      3) Asked to resign?
      4) Reinstated?

Administrative Jobs

These and like administrative jobs should be delegated to the superintendent of schools:

1. Advise the board of education as to the policies that should govern the suspension, retirement, resignation, and reinstatement of members of the instructional staff.
2. Accept or refuse resignations of members of the instructional staff.
3. Suspend, retire, and reinstate members of the instructional staff as the policies of the board require.
4. Keep adequate records of all matters pertaining to the suspension, resignation, retirement, and reinstatement of members of the instructional staff and submit appropriate reports thereof to the board of education.

PROBLEM OR JOB: SOLICITING SALES TO OR CONTRIBU-
TIONS FROM MEMBERS OF THE INSTRUCTIONAL
STAFF

Decisions made by a board of education on these and like
issues are its policies:

1. Soliciting sales:
   a. May outside solicitors interview members of the instructional staff on school premises for the purpose of
   selling them books, magazines, stocks, etc.?
2. Soliciting contributions:
   a. May members of the instructional staff while on school
   premises be canvassed for contributions to non-school
   causes?

Administrative Jobs

These and like administrative jobs should be delegated to the
superintendent of schools:

1. Admit or exclude solicitors.
2. Supervise all soliciting.
.3. Grant or deny requests for permission to solicit sales or
   contributions in accordance with the policies of the board.
4. Keep adequate records of all matters pertaining to the
   soliciting of sales to or contributions from members of the
   instructional staff and submit appropriate reports thereof
   to the board of education.

———

PROBLEM OR JOB: PHYSICAL EDUCATION AND HEALTH
SERVICE

Decisions made by a board of education on these and like
issues are its policies:

1. Services:
   a. What services shall the physical education and health
   department provide?
2. Organization:
   a. How shall the physical education and health service be
   organized?
   b. What shall be the relation of the physical education
   and health service to other divisions of the public schools?

3. Personnel:
   a. Qualifications:
      1) What shall be the qualifications with respect to the factors given under Qualifications of Members of Instructional Staff, page 73.
         a) Of the director?
         b) Of physicians?
         c) Of dentists?
         d) Of nurses?
   b. Selection and employment:
      1) Shall the persons nominated by the superintendent of schools for positions in the physical education and health service be approved?
   c. Duties and responsibilities:
      1) See the Work of Members of the Instructional Staff, page 73.
   d. Contracts:
      1) See Contracts with Members of the Instructional Staff, page 75.
   e. Assignment and transfer:
      1) See Assignment and Transfer of Members of the Instructional Staff, page 77.
   f. Leave of absence:
      1) See Leave of Absence of Members of the Instructional Staff, page 78.
   g. Attendance at professional meetings:
      1) See Attendance of Employees at Professional Meetings and Conventions, page 82.
   h. Salary schedules:
      1) See Salary Schedule of Instructional Staff, page 83.
   i. Transportation:
      1) See Transportation for Members of the Instructional Staff, page 85.
   j. Pensions and retirement funds:
      1) See Pensions and Retirement Funds for Members of Instructional Staff, page 86.
   k. Suspension, resignation, retirement, and reinstatement:
      1) See Suspension, Resignation, Retirement and Reinstatement of Members of Instructional Staff, page 87.

    l. Soliciting sales to or contributions from:
        1) See Soliciting Sales to or Contributions from Members of Instructional Staff, page 88.
  4. Appropriations:
    a. What shall be the annual appropriation for physical education and health service?

Administrative Jobs

These and like administrative jobs should be delegated to the superintendent of schools:

1. Advise the board of education as to the services that the physical education and health department should render.
2. Organize the physical education and health service in accordance with the policies of the board.
3. Ascertain the annual appropriation needed for the physical education and health department.
4. See the topics under Instructional Staff, beginning on the pages noted above.

PROBLEM OR JOB: STENOGRAPHIC AND CLERICAL SERVICE

Decisions made by a board of education on these and like issues are its policies:

1. For whom:
    a. What stenographic and clerical service shall be provided for:
        1) Board of education?
        2) Superintendent of schools?
        3) Assistant superintendents?
        4) Education Division
            a) Supervisors?
            b) Principals?
            c) Heads of departments.
        5) The Business Division
            a) Treasurer?
            b) Supervisor of buildings and grounds?
            c) Purchasing agent?
        6) Research Division?
        7) Physical education and health service?

      8) Legal Department?

      9) Attendance Department?

2. Personnel:

  a. Qualifications:

      1) What shall be the qualifications of the different stenographic and clerical workers with respect to the factors given under Qualifications of Members of Instructional Staff, page 73?

  b. Selection and employment:

      1) Shall the persons nominated by the superintendent of schools for stenographic and clerical positions be approved?

  c. Duties and responsibilities:

      1) See Work of Members of the Instructional Staff, page 73.

  d. Contracts:

      1) See Contracts with Members of the Instructional Staff, page 75.

  e. Assignments and transfer:

      1) See Assignment and Transfer of Members of the Instructional Staff, page 77.

  f. Leave of absence:

      1) See Leave of Absence for Members of the Instructional Staff, page 78.

  g. Attendance at professional meetings:

      1) See Attendance of Employees at Professional Meetings and Conventions, page 82.

  h. Salary schedule:

      1) See Salary Schedule of Instructional Staff, page 83.

  i. Transportation:

      1) See Transportation for Members of the Instructional Staff, page 85.

  j. Pensions and retirement funds:

      1) See Pensions and Retirement Funds for Members of the Instructional Staff, page 86.

  k. Suspension, resignation, retirement, and reinstatement:

      1) See Suspension, Resignation, Retirement, and Reinstatement of Members of Instructional Staff, page 87.

  l. Soliciting sales to or contributions from:

1) See Soliciting Sales to or Contributions from Members of Instructional Staff, page 88.
4. Appropriations:
   a. What shall be the annual appropriation for stenographic and clerical services for each person, department, and division listed in 1) above?

Administrative Jobs

These and like administrative jobs should be delegated to the superintendent of schools:
1. Advise the board of education as to the stenographic and clerical service required in the different offices of the school system.
2. Ascertain the annual appropriation needed for stenographic and clerical service.
3. See the topics under Instructional Staff beginning on the pages noted above.
4. Keep adequate records of all matters pertaining to stenographic and clerical service and submit appropriate reports thereof to the board of education.

PROBLEM OR JOB: HISTORY AND ANNIVERSARIES OF THE DISTRICT

Decisions made by a board of education on these and like issues are its policies:
1. Provisions for history:
   a. What provisions shall be made for the recording and printing of the history of the district?
2. Anniversaries:
   a. What anniversaries of the district shall be celebrated?
   b. How shall such anniversaries be celebrated?
3. Appropriations:
   a. What shall be the appropriation for
      1) Recording and printing the history of the district?
      2) The celebration of the district anniversaries?

Administrative Jobs

These and like administrative jobs should be delegated to the superintendent of schools:

1. Advise the board of education relative to the preparation of a desirable history of the district.
2. Have prepared and printed such history of the district as the board policies require.
3. Prepare such programs for the celebration of anniversaries of the district as the board authorizes.
4. Ascertain the appropriation needed for the preparation and printing of the district history and for the celebration of district anniversaries.
5. Keep adequate records of all matters pertaining to the history and anniversaries of the district and submit appropriate reports thereof to the board of education.

PROBLEM OR JOB: DISTRICT BOUNDARIES

Decisions made by a board of education on these and like issues are its policies:

1. Boundary lines within district:
    a. What shall be the boundary lines for the respective schools within the district?
    b. Under what conditions shall these boundary lines be changed?
2. Boundary lines of district:
    a. Shall the boundary lines of the district be changed by
        1) Addition of more territory?
        2) Withdrawal of territory within the district to other districts?
    b. Under what conditions shall such changes be made in the boundary lines.

Administrative Jobs

These and like administrative jobs should be delegated to the superintendent of schools:

1. Advise the board of education as to the policies that should govern the establishment of boundary lines of schools within the district.
2. Do the same for the district boundary lines.
3. Make such changes in boundary lines as the board authorizes.
4. Keep adequate records of the district boundaries and submit appropriate reports thereof to the board of education.

PROBLEM OR JOB: SELECTION OF GROUNDS

Decisions made by a board of education on these and like issues are its policies:

1. Bases for:
    a. What factors shall be considered in the selection of grounds for
        1) Sites for the different kinds of buildings?
        2) Playgrounds?
        3) Athletic fields?
        4) Gardens?
        5) Storage space?
        6) Parking space?

Administrative Jobs

These and like administrative jobs should be delegated to the superintendent of schools:

1. Advise the board of education as to the factors that should be considered in the selection of grounds for the different purposes.
2. Recommend specific pieces of land that should be acquired for school purposes.

PROBLEM OR JOB: ACQUISITION OF GROUNDS

Decisions made by a board of education on these and like issues are its policies:

1. How:
    a. Which of the following means shall be made use of in the acquisition of grounds:
        1) Options?
        2) Exercise of the right of eminent domain?
        3) Purchase?
        4) Exchange?
2. Specific grounds to be acquired:
    a. Shall the specific parcels of land recommended by the superintendent of schools be acquired by the means and at the cost recommended?
3. Appropriations:
    a. What shall be the annual appropriation for the acquisition of grounds?

Administrative Jobs

These and like administrative jobs should be delegated to the superintendent of schools:

1. Acquire parcels of land at the prices and by the means authorized by the board.
2. Ascertain the annual appropriation needed for the acquisition of grounds.
3. Keep adequate records of acquisition of grounds and submit appropriate reports thereof to the board of education.

PROBLEM OR JOB: IMPROVEMENT AND MAINTENANCE OF GROUNDS

Decisions made by a board of education on these and like issues are its policies:

1. Appropriations:
    a. What shall be the annual appropriation for the improvement and maintenance of grounds?
2. Recommendations:
    a. Shall the recommendations of the superintendent of schools relative to the improvement and maintenance of the respective grounds be approved?

Administrative Jobs

These and like administrative jobs should be delegated to the superintendent of schools:

1. Determine the desirable and needed improvements for the different grounds.
2. Ascertain the appropriation needed for making such desirable and needed improvements of grounds.
3. Ascertain the appropriation needed for the operation and maintenance of grounds.
4. Advise the board of education as to the improvement that should be made on the respective grounds.
5. Maintain the different grounds as the policies of the board require.
6. Make such improvements of the respective grounds as are authorized by the board of education.
7. Keep adequate records of all matters pertaining to the

improvement and maintenance of grounds and submit appropriate reports thereof to the board of education.

———

PROBLEM OR JOB: SALE OF BUILDINGS AND GROUNDS

Decisions made by a board of education on these and like issues are its policies:

1. Reasons:
   a. For what reasons shall school buildings and grounds be sold?
2. Procedure:
   a. Through what procedure shall the sale of buildings and grounds take place?
3. Recommendations:
   a. Shall the recommendations of the superintendent of schools relative to the sale of buildings and grounds be approved?
4. Income:
   a. Into what fund shall incomes from the sale of buildings and grounds be placed?
5. Failure to fulfill contract:
   a. Suppose that either the board or the purchaser is unable to fulfill the terms of the sale contract, what steps shall be taken by the board?

Administrative Jobs

These and like administrative jobs should be delegated to the superintendent of schools:

1. Advise the board of education as to the reasons for which buildings and grounds should be sold.
2. Recommend the sale of particular buildings and grounds.
3. Sell such buildings and grounds as the board authorizes and in the way the board authorizes.
4. Deposit the income from sales in such funds as the policies of the board require.
5. Carry out the policies of the board in case either party is unable to carry out the terms of the sale contract.
6. Keep adequate records of sales of buildings and grounds and submit appropriate reports thereof to the board of education.

PROBLEM OR JOB: SIGNS ON BUILDINGS AND GROUNDS

Decisions made by a board of education on this and like issues are its policies:

1. Kind permitted:
   a. What type of signs may be placed on school buildings and grounds?

Administrative Jobs

This and like administrative jobs should be delegated to the superintendent of schools:

1. Grant and deny requests for permission to place signs on school buildings and grounds.

———

PROBLEM OR JOB: NAMES OF BUILDINGS AND GROUNDS

Decisions made by a board of education on these and like issues are its policies:

1. How selected:
   a. How shall names for buildings and grounds be chosen?
2. How changed:
   a. Under what conditions shall the names of school buildings and grounds be changed?
3. Approval:
   a. Shall names for buildings and grounds proposed by superintendent of schools be approved?

Administrative Jobs

These and like administrative jobs should be delegated to the superintendent of schools:

1. Advise the board of desired changes in names of buildings and grounds.
2. Recommend names for buildings and grounds.

———

PROBLEM OR JOB: ENVIRONMENT OF SCHOOL BUILDINGS AND GROUNDS

Decisions made by a board of education on these and like issues are its policies:

1. Present undesirable environment:

    a. Suppose some school buildings and grounds are located in an undesirable environment, what shall be done to improve the situation?

2. Encroachment of undesirable businesses:
    a. What action shall be taken to prevent undesirable businesses from locating near school buildings and grounds?

3. Appropriations:
    a. What shall be the annual appropriation for maintaining and improving the environment of school buildings and grounds?

Administrative Jobs

These and like administrative jobs should be delegated to the superintendent of schools:

1. Advise the board of education on the activities threatening desirable environments of school buildings and grounds.
2. Take such measures as the policies of the board require to maintain and improve the environment of school buildings and grounds.
3. Ascertain the annual appropriation required for this purpose.
4. Keep adequate records of all matters pertaining to environment of school buildings and grounds and submit appropriate reports thereof to the board of education.

Problem or Job: ABANDONMENT OF BUILDINGS AND GROUNDS

Decisions made by a board of education on this and like issues are its policies:

1. Buildings to be abandoned:
    a. What buildings and grounds shall be abandoned?

Administrative Jobs

These and like administrative jobs should be delegated to the superintendent of schools:

1. Collect and organize adequate data for the board to determine intelligently whether or not certain buildings and grounds should be abandoned.

2. Make arrangements for the abandonment of such buildings and grounds as the board authorizes.

PROBLEM OR JOB: ACCESSIBILITY OF BUILDINGS AND GROUNDS

Decisions made by a board of education on these and like issues are its policies:

1. Problem:

   a. What action shall be taken if a school building is comparatively inaccessible to pupils because of
   1) Railroad tracks?
   2) Unbridged or poorly bridged canyons or streams?
   3) Inadequate transportation facilities?
   4) Distance pupils live from building?

2. Appropriations:

   a. What shall be the annual appropriation to keep buildings accessible to pupils?

Administrative Jobs

These and like administrative jobs should be delegated to the superintendent of schools:

1. Determine the accessibility of the respective buildings and grounds.
2. Prepare reports on the accessibility of buildings and grounds, and submit these to the board of education with recommendations as to (a) how buildings can be made more accessible, (b) whether certain buildings and sites should be abandoned.
3. Prepare estimates of the cost of making buildings and grounds more accessible.
4. Submit these to the board of education.
5. Carry out the decisions of the board of education with respect to making buildings and grounds more accessible.
6. Have buildings and grounds abandoned in accordance with the decisions of the school board.
7. Keep the board of education informed as to what is done to improve and maintain the proper accessibility of school buildings and grounds.

PROBLEM OR JOB: ADEQUACY OF BUILDINGS

Decisions made by a board of education on this and like issues are its policies:

1. If one or more of the present buildings are inadequate with respect to one or more of the following, what shall be done to improve the situation?

    a. Classrooms
    b. Laboratories
    c. Shops
    d. Auditorium
    e. Gymnasium
    f. Play rooms
    g. Cafeteria and lunch rooms
    h. Library
    i. Office space
    j. Baths
    k. Toilets
    l. Swimming pool
    m. Teachers' rest rooms
    n. Teachers' lunchrooms
    o. Corridors
    p. Stairways
    q. Elevators
    r. Fire escapes
    s. Storage space for
        1) Fuel
        2) Supplies and equipment
        3) Bicycles
    t. Janitors' rooms
    u. Blackboards
    v. Bulletin boards

Administrative Jobs

These and like administrative jobs should be delegated to the superintendent of schools:

1. Determine the adequacy of each of the school buildings with respect to the factors listed under 1 above.
2. Conduct a permanent and continuing study of the school building situation.
3. Prepare from time to time appropriate reports of the adequacy

of the different factors in the school building situation and submit these to the board of education with recommendations as to how it can and should be improved.

———

PROBLEM OR JOB: ALTERATION (INCLUDING ADDITIONS) AND REPAIR OF BUILDINGS

Decisions made by a board of education on these and like issues are its policies:

1. Alterations and repairs:
   a. What alterations and repairs shall be made in each of the following in each building?
      1) Classrooms
      2) Laboratories
      3) Shops
      4) Auditorium
      5) Gymnasium
      6) Play rooms
      7) Cafeteria and lunchrooms
      8) Library
      9) Office space
      10) Baths
      11) Toilets
      12) Swimming pool
      13) Teachers' rest rooms
      14) Teachers' lunchrooms
      15) Corridors
      16) Stairways
      17) Elevators
      18) Fire escapes
      19) Storage space for
         a) Fuel
         b) Supplies and equipment
         c) Bicycles
      20) Janitors' rooms
      21) Foundations
      22) Walls
      23) Floors
      24) Ceilings
      25) Roofs

26) Doors
27) Windows
28) Lightning rods
29) Plastering
30) Color scheme
31) Blackboards
32) Bulletin boards
33) Acoustics
34) Lighting
35) Heating
36) Ventilation
37) Plumbing

2. Appropriations for alterations and repairs:
   a. What shall be the annual appropriation for alterations and repairs?
   b. What shall be the appropriation for each job of alteration or repair?
3. Financing of alterations and repairs:
   a. What alterations and repairs shall be financed from bond money in the Building Fund and what ones shall be paid from tax money?
4. Qualifications of persons or companies making alterations:
   a. What shall be the qualifications of persons or companies making alterations?
5. Basis of selection of persons or companies making alterations and repairs:
   a. What shall be the basis for selecting the persons or companies to make alterations and repairs?

Administrative Jobs

These and like administrative jobs should be delegated to the superintendent of schools:

1. Determine the exact condition in each building of each item in 1 above.
2. Determine what alterations and repairs are desirable.
3. Ascertain the cost of such alterations and repairs.
4. Prepare and submit to the board of education adequate and suitable reports on
   a. The need for alterations and repairs.

    b. The approximate cost of such alterations and repairs.

    c. The alterations and repairs that have been made.

    d. By whom these have been made.

    e. At what cost they have been made.

5. Prepare plans and specifications of alterations and repairs authorized by the board of education.

6. Select and employ, in accordance with the policies of the school board, persons or companies to make the alterations and repairs authorized by the board of education.

7. See to it that the alterations and repairs are made in accordance with the terms of the plans and specifications embodied in the contract.

8. Accept or reject the bonds required of the persons and companies awarded contracts to make alterations and repairs.

9. Pay the persons and companies making alterations and repairs in accordance with the terms of the contract.

10. Keep adequate records of all matters pertaining to alterations and repairs and submit suitable reports thereof to the board of education.

PROBLEM OR JOB: NEW BUILDINGS

Decisions made by a board of education on these and like issues are its policies:

1. Number and type:

    a. What buildings shall be constructed?

2. Appropriations:

    a. What shall be the total appropriations for these buildings?

3. Location:

    a. What shall be the site of each new building?

4. Orientation:

    a. What shall be the orientation of each new building?

5. Size and shape:

    a. What pupils and how many shall each new building be built to accommodate?

    b. What rooms shall there be in each new building?

    c. What shall be the dimensions and shape of each new building?

6. Arrangement, size, and shape of rooms and corridors:
   a. What shall be the arrangement of rooms and corridors?
   b. What shall be the size and shape of the respective rooms and corridors?

7. Materials of construction:
   a. Of what material shall each part of new buildings be constructed?
   b. What shall be the total appropriation for materials for each building?
   c. Shall materials be purchased from local firms provided it can be secured from them at as good prices as from non-local dealers?
   d. Under what conditions may substitutions be made in the building material?

8. Service systems:
   a. What heating, ventilation, lighting, plumbing, and cleaning systems shall be installed in each new building.
   b. What shall be the appropriation for each of these for each building?

9. Color scheme and decorations:
   a. What shall be the color scheme and decorations of each new building?
   b. What shall be the appropriation for these purposes for each building?

10. Equipment:
    a. What equipment shall be installed in each new building?
    b. What shall be the appropriation for the equipment of each building?
    c. Shall equipment be purchased from local firms provided it can be secured from them at as good prices as from non-local dealers?
    d. Under what conditions may substitutions be made in the building equipment?

11. Memorial features:
    a. What memorial features shall be made a part of each new building?
    b. Shall a tablet or a panel bearing the names of the members of the board of education, and others be placed in new buildings?
    c. If so, where shall such tablets or panels be placed?

d. What publicity shall be given to the installation of memorials in new buildings?

e. What appropriation shall be made for memorial features?

f. See Gifts to Schools, page 139.

12. Plans and specifications:

a. Shall the plans and specifications prepared by the architect and approved by the superintendent of schools be adopted?

b. What changes may be made in the plans and specifications after their adoption?

13. Laying of cornerstone and dedication:

a. How shall each of these events in the construction of new buildings be celebrated?

b. What appropriation shall be made for such events?

c. What inscription shall be placed on the cornerstone of each building?

14. Cost:

a. What shall be the total cost of each new building fully equipped?

Administrative Jobs

These and like administrative jobs should be delegated to the superintendent of schools:

1. Ascertain the new buildings needed and advise the board thereof.

2. Determine the appropriation needed for each of the buildings to be constructed.

3. Advise the board of education on all matters analyzed under 3 to 12, inclusive, above.

4. Carry out the decisions of the school board on each of these matters.

———

Problem or Job: THE ARCHITECT

Decisions made by a board of education on these and like issues are its policies:

1. Qualifications:

a. What shall be the qualifications of the architect with respect to

1) Age?

2) Training?
3) Experience?
   a) As a general architect.
   b) As a school architect.
4) Residence?

2. Selection:
  a. By what procedure shall the selection of the architect be made?
  b. Shall the architect selected by the superintendent of schools be approved?

3. Duties and responsibilities:
  a. What shall be the architect's duties and responsibilities with respect to:
    1) Preparation and adoption of the plans and specifications?
    2) Selection of the general and the subsidiary contractors?
    3) Making and enforcing building and equipment contracts?
    4) Selection of material?
    5) Supervision of the construction of the building and the selection and installation of equipment?
    6) "Extras" added to plans and specifications
      a) After plans and specifications have been adopted by the board of education?
      b) After the contracts have been let?
    7) Other changes in the plans and specifications
      a) After the contracts have been let?
      b) After the construction has been started?
      c) In the equipment after it has been purchased or delivered?
      d) In equipment after its installation has been started?
    8) Payment of building estimates?
    9) Acceptance of buildings and equipment?

4. Compensation:
  a. What shall be the remuneration of the architect in case his plans and specifications are
    1) Rejected?
    2) Accepted?
  b. From what fund shall the architect's fees be paid?
  c. When shall the architect be paid?

Administrative Jobs

These and like administrative jobs should be delegated to the superintendent of schools.

1. Advise the board of education as to qualifications of school architects.
2. Select the architect and submit such nomination to the board of education for its approval.
3. Prepare and submit to the architect the data and information necessary for the preparation of plans and specifications.
4. See to it that the architect performs his duties and responsibilities in accordance with terms of his contract.
5. Pay the architect.
6. Keep adequate records of all matters pertaining to the architect and submit suitable reports thereof to the board of education.

Problem or Job: CONSULTING ARCHITECTS

Decisions made by a board of education on these and like issues are its policies:

1. For issues on Qualifications, Selection, Duties and Responsibilities, and Compensation, see Architect, page 105.
2. Relation to regular architect:
   a. What shall be the relation of the consulting architects to the regular architect?

Administrative Jobs

These and like administrative jobs should be delegated to the superintendent of schools.

See Architect, page 105.

Problem or Job: BUILDING CONTRACTORS AND SUB-CONTRACTORS

Decisions made by a board of education on these and like issues are its policies:

1. Qualifications:
   a. What shall be the qualifications of the contractor with respect to

       1) Age?
       2) Training?
       3) Experience?
          a) As a general contractor.
          b) As a school contractor.
       4) Residence?
  2. Selection:
    a. By what procedure shall the contractor be selected?
    b. Shall the contractor selected by the superintendent of schools be approved?
  3. Duties and responsibilities:
    a. What shall be the duties and responsibilities of the respective contractors relative to
       1) Selection of subcontractors?
       2) Selection and purchase of building material and equipment?
       3) Substitution of building material and equipment?
       4) Date of completion of buildings?
       5) Employment of local labor?
       6) Strikes of laborers employed?
       7) Payment of labor employed?
       8) Payment for material and equipment purchased?
       9) Defective material, equipment, and workmanship?
  4. Contract:
    a. Form and content:
       1) What shall be the form and content of contracts with the different building contractors employed?
    b. Violation:
       1) What shall be the penalty for a contractor's failure to perform each duty and to satisfy each responsibility set forth in his contract?
       2) How shall such penalties be enforced?
  5. Bonds:
    a. What bonds shall the respective contractors provide?
  6. Payment:
    a. When and in what amounts shall the contractors be paid?

Administrative Jobs

These and like administrative jobs should be delegated to the superintendent of schools:

1. Advise the board of education as to the qualifications of contractors.
2. Select the contractors and submit such nominations to the board of education for its approval.
3. See to it that the contractors perform their duties and responsibilities in accordance with the terms of their contracts.
4. Enforce the penalties provided by the policies of the board in cases of violation of contracts by contractors.
5. Pay contractors.
6. Approve or reject contractors' bonds in accordance with the policies of the board.
7. Keep adequate records of all matters pertaining to the contractors and submit suitable reports thereof to the board of education.

PROBLEM OR JOB: ACCEPTANCE OF BUILDINGS

Decisions made by a board of education on these and like issues are its policies:

1. Use of buildings before their acceptance:
   a. Under what conditions shall the superintendent make arrangements for the use of buildings before they are definitely accepted by the district?
2. Conditions to be satisfied before buildings are accepted:
   a. What conditions must be satisfied before buildings may be accepted from a general contractor?

Administrative Jobs

These and like administrative jobs should be delegated to the superintendent of schools:

1. Advise the board of education as to the conditions that should be satisfied before a building is accepted.
2. Determine when such conditions have been met.
3. Make arrangements with the general contractors for such use of buildings before they are completed as designated by the board and on such conditions as the policies of the board require.
4. Accept buildings from the general contractors.
5. Keep adequate records of all matters pertaining to the

acceptance of buildings and submit appropriate reports thereof to the board of education.

———

Problem or Job: FIRE RISK

Decisions made by a board of education on these and like issues are its policies:

1. Annual appropriation to reduce fire risk:
   a. What shall be the annual appropriation to reduce the fire risk in the public schools?
2. Decrease in fire risk:
   a. Shall fire risk in the respective buildings be reduced by
      1) The purchase and installation of fire extinguishers?
      2) The inspection and refilling of chemical fire extinguishers?
      3) The painting of fire exit signs?
      4) The installation, alteration, or repair of fire escapes?
      5) The storage of fuel in bins made of indestructible material?
      6) The storage of sweeping compound and other highly combustible material in metal containers?
      7) The frequent inspection of the electric wiring?
      8) The installation and repair of panic bolts?
      9) The inspection of exits at frequent intervals in order to make sure that these are kept unlocked and unobstructed in accordance with fire regulations?
      10) The regular inspection of boilers and chimneys?
      11) The alteration and repair of boilers and chimneys whenever the fire hazard can thereby be reduced?
      12) The inspection of buildings at frequent intervals to prevent the accumulation of inflammable material contrary to fire regulations?
      13) The frequent observance of fire drills?
      14) The frequent inspection of the fire alarm systems?
      15) The observance of Fire Prevention Week?
      16) The installation of lightning rods?

Administrative Jobs

These and like administrative jobs should be delegated to the superintendent of schools:

1. Determine the amount needed annually to keep the fire risk at the minimum.
2. Advise the board of education as to means of reducing the fire risk in each building.
3. Reduce the fire risk by each of the above means authorized by the board of education.
4. Keep adequate records of all matters pertaining to fire risks and keep the board of education informed concerning the situation in the respective buildings.

––––––––

PROBLEM OR JOB: INSURANCE ON BUILDINGS AND EQUIPMENT

Decisions made by a board of education on these and like issues are its policies:

1. Insurance against loss from fire and wind:
    a. Shall the buildings and equipment belonging to the district be insured against loss from fire and wind?
    b. Shall the school district carry its own insurance by establishing and maintaining a fund calculated to be sufficiently great to meet all losses from fire and wind?
2. Appraisal of buildings and equipment:
    a. How shall the valuation of buildings and equipment be determined for purposes of insurance?
3. Insurance rates:
    a. How shall the rates of insurance on the different buildings and their equipment be determined?
4. Qualifications of insurance companies:
    a. What shall be the qualifications of the companies with whom insurance is placed?
5. Term of insurance:
    a. For how long periods shall the different buildings and their equipment be insured?
6. Renewal of policies:
    a. When insurance policies expire, what rules shall govern their renewal?
7. Insurance of buildings being constructed:
    a. Shall buildings in the process of construction be insured by the school district?

Administrative Jobs

These and like administrative jobs should be delegated to the superintendent of schools:

1. Appraise buildings and equipment.
2. Ascertain rates of insurance.
3. Place insurance in accordance with policies of the school board with companies having the qualifications designated by the board of education.
4. Pay insurance premiums.
5. Have permits for the storage of inflammable material attached to policies.
6. Keep check on the insurance term schedule and renew policies in accordance with the policies of the board of education.
7. Keep adequate records on all matters pertaining to the insurance of buildings and equipment and keep the board of education adequately informed about them.

PROBLEM OR JOB: SETTLEMENT WITH INSURANCE COMPANIES FOR LOSS OF BUILDINGS AND EQUIPMENT

Decisions made by a board of education on this and like issues are its policies:

1. Procedure:
    a. How shall the school district proceed to secure settlement with insurance companies for buildings destroyed by fire or wind?

Administrative Jobs

These and like administrative jobs should be delegated to the superintendent of schools:

1. Appraise the loss incurred.
2. Ascertain the amount due from the insurance companies.
3. In case of disagreement with the insurance companies as to the amount due, secure an appraisal of the loss and of the amount due the district.
4. When satisfied that the amount of the loss has been correctly determined, collect this amount from the insurance companies.

5. Deposit the money so collected in the proper funds.
6. Keep complete records on all matters pertaining to losses from fire and wind, and submit suitable reports thereof to the board of education.

PROBLEM OR JOB: HEATING AND VENTILATION IN NEW BUILDINGS

Decisions made by a board of education on these and like issues are its policies:

1. System to be installed:
   a. What system of heating and ventilation shall be installed in new buildings?
2. Automatic temperature control:
   a. Shall automatic temperature regulation system be installed?
3. Appropriation:
   a. What amount shall be appropriated for the heating and ventilation equipment and its installation?
4. Awarding contracts:
   a. Shall the contracts for the installation of heating and ventilation equipment be awarded on the basis of competitive bids?
   b. What shall be the qualifications of the bidder to whom such contracts shall be awarded?

Administrative Jobs

These and like administrative jobs should be delegated to the superintendent of schools:

1. Prepare plans and specifications of the heating and ventilation equipment to be installed.
2. Secure bids for the equipment to be installed.
3. Accept or reject bids for equipment and its installation.
4. Award contracts for equipment and its installation.
5. Prepare the contracts for the purchase of equipment and its installation.
6. Check on the equipment delivered and its installation and secure rigid adherence to the plans and specifications.
7. Make payments in accordance with the terms of the contract.
8. Keep proper records of the purchase and installation of this

equipment and submit appropriate reports to the board of education.

PROBLEM OR JOB: OPERATION OF HEATING AND VENTILA-
TION SYSTEMS

Decisions made by a board of education on these and like issues are its policies:

1. Temperature and humidity to be maintained:
   a. What temperature and humidity shall be maintained in school buildings while they are in use?
2. Cost of operation:
   a. Shall a new type of grate and blower be installed in some buildings to determine if the use of slack will reduce the heating costs?
   b. Shall a suitable type of equipment be installed in some buildings to ascertain the comparative cost of oil and coal as fuels?

Administrative Jobs

These and like administrative jobs should be delegated to the superintendent of schools:

1. Maintain the right temperature and humidity in all parts of school buildings.
2. See to it that furnaces are properly stoked.
3. See to it that ventilating systems are correctly operated.
4. Ascertain the kind of coal best adapted to the heating systems in use.
5. Determine whether or not the use of oil or slack will reduce heating and ventilation costs.
6. Keep an adequate record of the cost of operating the heating and ventilation systems of the respective buildings.
7. Make appropriate reports to the board of education.

PROBLEM OR JOB: REPLACEMENT AND REPAIR OF HEAT-
ING AND VENTILATION SYSTEMS

Decisions made by a board of education on this and like issues are its policies:

1. Annual appropriation:

    a. What appropriation shall be made each year for replacement and repair of heating and ventilation systems?

2. Awarding contracts:

    a. Shall all replacement and repair jobs be awarded on the basis of competitive bids?

    b. What shall be the qualifications of the bidder to whom such contracts shall be awarded?

Administrative Jobs

These and like administrative jobs should be delegated to the superintendent of schools:

1. Determine the efficiency of the heating and ventilation equipment in the respective buildings.
2. Determine what heating and ventilation equipment in the respective buildings should be replaced or repaired.
3. Determine the cost of replacing and repairing this equipment.
4. Secure bids for replacing and repairing this equipment.
5. Accept or reject bids for replacing and repairing such equipment.
6. Award contracts for the replacement and repair of this equipment.
7. Approve or reject the bonds of the contractor awarded such contracts.
8. Inspect the workmanship and the material in the making of these replacements and repairs.
9. Accept or reject the replacements and repairs made.
10. Inspect the boilers.
11. Make payments for replacements and repairs.
12. Keep the necessary records and make adequate reports to the board of education.

PROBLEM OR JOB: LEASING OF BUILDINGS AND ROOMS
FOR SCHOOL PURPOSES

1. Purposes for which leased:

    a. What shall determine whether buildings and rooms may or shall be leased by the district for each of the following uses:

      1) Assembly halls?

      2) Auditoriums?
      3) Athletics?
      4) Classrooms?
      5) Gymnasiums?
      6) Laboratories?
      7) Libraries?
      8) Offices?
      9) Play rooms?

2. Rent for buildings and rooms:
   a. What shall determine the rent that may be paid for buildings and rooms for each of the above purposes?
3. Appropriations for rent:
   a. What shall be the annual appropriation for rent of buildings and rooms?
4. Period of lease:
   a. For what periods may leases on buildings and rooms be made?
5. Termination of leases:
   a. On what conditions may or shall such leases be terminated?

Administrative Jobs

These and like administrative jobs should be delegated to the superintendent of schools:

1. Determine the need for and the advisability of leasing buildings or rooms for district needs.
2. Secure leases on buildings and rooms needed on conditions in accordance with policies laid down by the board of education.
3. Renew leases.
4. Pay rent on buildings and rooms leased.
5. Advise the board of education as to annual appropriation needed for rents.
6. Terminate leases.
7. Keep adequate records on all matters pertaining to leasing of buildings and keep board of education informed thereon.

PROBLEM OR JOB: LEASING OF BUILDINGS OWNED BY DISTRICT

Decisions made by a board of education on these and like issues are its policies:

1. Leasing of buildings or lands purchased by district:
    a. Shall buildings or land purchased for school purposes be leased during the period between the purchase of such property and the beginning of construction of school buildings on such sites?
    b. For what purposes may such property be leased?
    c. On what terms may it be leased?
2. Leasing of abandoned district buildings:
    a. Under what conditions may abandoned school buildings be leased?
3. Rent from school property:
    a. Into what funds shall rent accruing from leases be placed?

Administrative Jobs

These and like administrative jobs should be delegated to the superintendent of schools:

1. Accept or reject offers to lease such property.
2. Prepare and sign contracts covering such leases.
3. Collect rents.
4. Place income from rents in funds designated by board of education.
5. Keep adequate records of all matters pertaining to leasing of buildings and prepare proper reports thereon for the board of education.

PROBLEM OR JOB: LIGHTING OF BUILDINGS AND GROUNDS

Decisions made by a board of education on these and like issues are its policies:

1. System of lighting in new buildings:
    a. What system of artificial lighting shall be installed in new buildings?
2. Appropriation for lighting equipment in new buildings:
    a. What shall be the appropriation for the lighting equipment for each new building?
3. Alterations and repairs of lighting systems:
    a. See Alteration and Repair of Buildings, page 101.
4. Use of artificial lighting:

  a. When and under what conditions may or shall artificial lighting of buildings and grounds be used?

5. Appropriations for artificial lighting:

  a. What shall be the annual appropriation for artificial lighting?

6. Sources of electric current and gas:

  a. What shall determine whether electric current and gas shall be purchased from the city or from public service corporations?

  b. If there is more than one public service corporation supplying electric current or gas, what shall determine from which company electric current and gas shall be purchased?

Administrative Jobs

These and like administrative jobs should be delegated to the superintendent of schools:

1. Advise board of education on the system of lighting that should be installed.
2. Determine the cost of the installation of lighting equipment.
3. Ascertain the annual appropriation needed for lighting.
4. See that artificial lighting is used in accordance with the policies of the school board.
5. Make alterations and repairs in lighting systems.
6. Purchase electric current and gas.
7. Pay for electric current and gas.
8. Keep adequate records on all matters pertaining to the lighting of buildings and keep the board of education duly informed thereon.

Problem or Job: MOVING BUILDINGS

Decisions made by a board of education on these and like issues are its policies:

1. Conditions on which buildings should be moved:

  a. Under what conditions shall buildings be moved?

2. Buildings to be moved:

  a. Shall buildings be moved as recommended by the superintendent of schools?

Administrative Jobs

These and like administrative jobs should be delegated to the superintendent of schools:

1. Advise the board of education as to the condition making it desirable to move buildings.
2. Make recommendations to the board relative to buildings that should be moved.
3. Make arrangements for the moving of buildings.
   a. Secure bids for.
   b. Accept or reject bids for.
   c. Award and sign contracts for moving of buildings.
   d. Accept or reject bonds of person or company moving building.
   e. Pay for moving building.
   f. Secure city permit for moving of buildings where necessary.
4. Keep adequate records of all matters pertaining to moving of buildings and submit suitable report thereof to the board of education.

———

PROBLEM OR JOB: SPECIAL USE OF GROUNDS, BUILDINGS, EQUIPMENT, AND SUPPLIES

Decisions made by a board of education on these and like issues are its policies:

1. Grounds, buildings, equipment, and supplies that may be used:
   a. Which of the following may be used for other than the regular work of the schools or at other than the regular school hours on school days?
      1) Classrooms
      2) Laboratories
      3) Shops
      4) Auditorium
      5) Gymnasium
      6) Play rooms
      7) Cafeteria and lunchrooms
      8) Library
      9) Offices
      10) Baths
      11) Toilets

12) Swimming pool
13) Teachers' rest rooms
14) Teachers' lunchrooms
15) Corridors
16) Playgrounds
17) Athletic fields
18) Tennis courts
19) Lawns
20) Schoolyards
21) Vacant lots owned by district
22) Stadium and grand stand
23) Band stand
24) Playground equipment
25) Laboratory and shop equipment
26) Athletic equipment
27) Office equipment
28) Lockers
29) Textbooks
30) Telephones

2. Purposes for which buildings may be used:

   a. For which of the following purposes may buildings be used?

1) Americanization work
2) Art exhibits
3) Athletic contests
4) Band practice
5) Banquets
6) Benefit programs
7) Card parties
8) Church choir practice
9) Church services
10) Community choruses
11) Community meetings
12) Concerts
13) Conventions
14) Dances
15) Debates
16) Dinners
17) District contests
18) Educational meetings

19) Foreign language instruction
20) Fruit canning centers
21) Health work
22) Instruction in regular school subjects
23) Instruction for:
    a) Blind persons
    b) Deaf persons
    c) Crippled persons
    d) Persons who are ailing physically
24) Laboratory instruction for nurses training in hospitals
25) Lecture courses
26) Luncheons
27) Lodge meetings
28) Moving pictures
29) Musicales
30) Orchestra practice
31) Patriotic meetings
    a) For celebration of American ideals and events
    b) For celebration of ideals and events of foreign nations
32) Political meetings
33) Practice for athletic contests
34) Recreation in form of games and sports
35) Religious instruction
36) Religious meetings
37) State contests
38) Style shows
39) Teachers' examinations
40) Teachers' meetings
41) Theatrical productions
42) Theatrical rehearsals
43) Vegetable canning centers
44) Voting places

3. Who may use buildings:
    a. Which of the following may use public school buildings, grounds, and equipment?
        1) Art clubs
        2) Athletic associations

3) Bands
4) Boy Scouts
5) Business firms
6) Camp Fire Girls
7) Canning clubs
8) Catholic clubs
9) Children's saving societies
10) Chamber of commerce
11) Churches
12) Colleges
13) Concert companies
14) Debating societies
15) Dramatic societies
16) Educational associations
17) Foreign language groups
18) Garden clubs
19) Health organizations
20) Hebrew Young People's Association
21) Hospital training schools
22) Improvement leagues
23) Ku Klux Klan
24) Labor unions
25) Literary societies
26) Lodges
27) Orchestras
28) Organizations of public school pupils
29) Organizations such as Rotarians, Kiwanis, etc.
30) Orphanages
31) Parent-Teacher Associations
32) Playground associations
33) Political parties
34) Radio clubs
35) Recreation organizations
36) Red Cross
37) Religious organizations
38) Salvation Army
39) Sunday school associations
40) Sunday school classes
41) Teachers
42) United States Armory

    43) Visiting Nurses Associations
    44) Women's clubs
    45) Young Men's Christian Association
    46) Young Women's Christian Association

4. Use of district property by local and non-local persons or groups:
    a. In each of the preceding cases, what shall be the difference in the conditions on which local persons may secure the use of district property from those on which non-local persons or groups may secure the use of buildings?

5. Public versus non-public use of district property:
    a. In each of the preceding cases, what shall be the difference in the conditions on which the use of district property may be secured if the public is invited from those on which the use of district property may be secured if the public is excluded?

6. Use of district property by professionals and by non-professionals:
    a. In each of the preceding cases, what shall be the difference in the conditions on which professionals and non-professionals may secure the use of district property?

7. Sunday use of district property:
    a. For what purposes may the respective persons or groups listed under 3 above use district property on Sunday?

8. Conditions on which the use of district property may be granted:
    a. Requests for use:
        1) In what form shall they be made?
        2) How long in advance shall they be made?
    b. Rules governing use:
        1) What rules shall govern the special use of district property?
    c. Control:
        1) What shall be the control and supervision for carrying out the rules governing the special use of district property?
    d. Protection:
        1) How shall protection of public school property be guaranteed while property is used for special purposes?

  2) How shall responsibility for damage to property be located?
  e. Rent for the use of district property:
  1) What shall be the rent for the use of the different kinds of school property?
  2) Shall this rent be uniform
  a) For all persons or groups?
  b) Regardless of the purpose for which the property is used?
  c) Whether admission is or is not charged?
  d) Whether the proceeds are or are not used for charity or public purposes?
  3) When shall the rent be paid?
  4) Under what conditions shall rent be refunded?
  f. Janitor service:
  1) Who shall provide janitorial services when buildings are used for special purposes?
  2) Shall the regular janitors do the janitorial work?
  3) What shall be their remuneration for such services?
  4) How shall they be paid?
  g. Contract to be used:
  1) Shall the contract between the district and persons or groups using district property be oral or written?
  2) What shall be the form and content of such contracts?
  3) How long in advance of the time the district property is to be used is the contract to be made?
  h. Policing of school grounds:
  1) How shall the school grounds be policed during the time they are used?
  a) By non-school groups?
  i. Allocation of income from school property:
  1) Into what funds shall money be placed that is collected for the use of or for damage done to school property?

Administrative Jobs

These and like administrative jobs should be delegated to the superintendent of schools:
  1. Receive applications for the use of district property.
  2. Grant or refuse such applications.

3. Represent the district when contracts for the special use of district property are made.
4. Enforce the rules and regulations governing the special use of district property.
5. Collect damages done to district property while it is rented out.
6. Collect rent.
7. See that the required janitorial work is done when buildings are used for special purposes.
8. Pay janitors for this extra janitorial work.
9. Keep adequate records of all matters pertaining to the special use of buildings and submit suitable reports thereof to the board of education.
10. See also Athletic Fields and Stadia, page 34.

PROBLEM OR JOB: JANITORIAL SERVICE

Decisions made by a board of education on these and like issues are its policies:

1. Annual appropriations:
   a. How much shall be appropriated annually for janitorial service?
      1) For wages?
      2) For supplies and equipment?
   b. Contract:
      1) Under what conditions shall janitorial work be let on contract?
   c. Measurement:
      1) What shall be the units of measure for determining the size of the different janitorial jobs?

JANITORIAL WORKERS

1. Qualifications:
   a. What shall be the qualifications of janitorial workers of the different grades?
   b. Shall members of the regular janitorial staff be used when buildings are used by non-school groups?
2. Wages:
   a. What shall be the pay of janitorial workers on the different levels?

1) For regular work?
2) For extra work?

b. On what basis shall wage increases be granted janitorial workers?

c. What recognition shall be given janitorial workers for devotion to their work or for long and meritorious service?

3. Injuries:

a. What part of a janitorial worker's wages shall go on while he is absent because of injuries sustained in the performance of his duties?

b. For how long a period of absence due to this cause shall his wages go on?

c. Shall the school district pay any or all doctor bills, nurse bills, and hospital bills arising from injuries incurred by a janitorial worker in the discharge of his duties?

4. Insurance:

a. Shall the school district carry workingmen's compensation insurance for its janitorial workers? If so, how much?

b. What shall be the qualifications of the companies with which such insurance is placed?

5. Conduct:

a. May janitorial workers smoke or use profane language while on duty?

6. Leaves of absence:

a. Shall a janitorial worker be granted leave of absence
1) On account of illness
a) Of himself?
b) Of a member of his immediate family?
c) Of a distant relative?
d) Of a friend?
2) On account of death
a) Of a member of his immediate family?
b) Of a distant relative?
c) Of a friend?
3) For vacation?

b. Under what conditions may a janitorial worker leave his work before the end of the day or the end of the term?

c. For how long a period may a janitorial worker be granted leave of absence?

    d. Under what conditions may a leave of absence be extended?

    e. At what intervals may a janitorial worker be granted leave of absence?

    f. What part of a janitorial worker's wages shall be paid him while he is on leave of absence?

    g. What shall be the penalty for failure of a janitorial worker to report for duty immediately upon the expiration of his leave of absence?

    h. What shall be the penalty for using a leave of absence for a different purpose than that for which it is granted?

7. Retirement:

    a. Under what conditions shall janitors be retired?

    b. Shall a pension or retirement fund for janitorial workers be established or maintained?

    c. What rules shall govern the administration of such a pension or retirement fund?

Administrative Jobs

These and like administrative jobs should be delegated to the superintendent of schools:

1. Select janitorial workers.
2. Hire janitorial workers.
3. Assign janitorial workers to buildings and jobs.
4. Transfer janitorial workers.
5. Suspend janitorial workers.
6. Dismiss janitorial workers.
7. Accept or reject resignations of janitorial workers.
8. Grant or deny requests for leaves of absence to janitorial workers.
9. Contract for janitorial services as the policies of the board require.
10. Use such units of measure for determining the size of janitorial jobs as required by school board policies.
11. Allow or refuse payment of bills for doctor, nurse, or hospital service incurred by janitorial workers as a result of injuries sustained in the performance of their work.
12. Pay janitorial workers.
13. Purchase workingmen's compensation insurance for janitorial workers.

14. Supervise the payment of janitorial workers' claims for workingmen's compensation insurance.
15. See that janitorial workers perform their duties as required.
16. Issue supplies and equipment to janitorial workers.
17. Enforce all rules and regulations of the board of education pertaining to janitorial service.
18. Keep adequate records of all matters pertaining to janitorial service and submit appropriate reports thereof to the board of education.

———

PROBLEM OR JOB: COAL SUPPLY

Decisions made by a board of education on these and like issues are its policies:

1. From whom purchased:
   a. Shall coal always be purchased from the lowest bidder?
   b. Shall it be purchased from the local dealer submitting the lowest bid?
   c. Shall the coal contract be divided among the local dealers regardless of the bids they submit?
   d. If the bids are the same, shall the coal contract be awarded a single dealer or shall it be split among the several dealers?
   e. If the bids are the same and one dealer is to be awarded the contract, how shall he be selected?
2. How purchased:
   a. Shall coal be purchased on the basis of the number of heat units it contains?
   b. What weight shall be used?
      1) Mine weights?
      2) Dealer's weights?
      3) Bonded scales' weight?
      4) School weights?
   c. How shall the future coal supply outlook be considered when the purchase of coal is contemplated?
3. Storage:
   a. If the storage capacity is inadequate, may a part of the coal supply be stored outside?

Administrative Jobs

These and like administrative jobs should be delegated to the superintendent of schools:

1. Select the kind of coal to be used.
2. Determine the quantity of coal needed.
3. Purchase the coal.
   a. Call for bids.
   b. Accept or reject bids.
   c. Award contracts.
4. Delivery of coal:
   a. Determine when it is to be delivered.
   b. Determine where it is to be delivered.
   c. Determine how it is to be delivered.
   d. Check on the quality and the weight of coal when it is delivered.
5. Provide storage space for coal.
6. Pay for coal.
7. Maintain an adequate supply of coal at all times.
8. Keep adequate records of the coal purchased and used in the respective buildings.
9. Prepare and submit to the board of education appropriate reports of the coal purchased and used.

PROBLEM OR JOB: EQUIPMENT

Decisions made by a board of education on these and like issues are its policies:

1. Types or characteristics:
   a. What shall be the general type or characteristics of the equipment to be purchased and installed in the respective divisions of the school systems?
2. Appropriations:
   a. What shall be the appropriation for the purchase and installation of equipment in each new building?
   b. What shall be the annual appropriation for the alteration, repair, and replacement of equipment in the respective buildings?
   c. What shall be the annual appropriation for the purchase and installation of additional equipment in each building?

3. From whom purchased:
   a. What shall be the qualifications of the firms or persons from whom equipment is purchased?
4. Transfer, sale, and rent:
   a. Under what conditions shall equipment be transferred, sold, or rented?
5. Insurance:
   a. See Insurance of Buildings and Equipment, page 111.
6. Inventories:
   a. What inventories shall be made annually of school equipment?

Administrative Jobs

These and like administrative jobs should be delegated to the superintendent of schools:

1. Advise the board of education as to the desirable types or characteristics of equipment to be purchased and installed.
2. Ascertain the appropriation needed for
   a. Purchase and installation of equipment in new buildings.
   b. Alteration, repair, and maintenance of equipment in the respective buildings.
   c. Purchase and installation of additional equipment in the different buildings.
3. Select equipment.
4. Purchase equipment.
5. Install equipment.
6. Pay for equipment.
7. Repair and replace equipment.
8. Transfer equipment.
9. Rent equipment.
10. Sell equipment.
11. Insure equipment. (See Insurance of Buildings and Equipment, page 111.)
12. Make inventories of equipment.
13. Keep adequate records of all matters pertaining to equipment and submit appropriate reports thereof to the board of education.

PROBLEM OR JOB: EDUCATIONAL SUPPLIES

Decisions made by a board of education on these and like issues are its policies:

1. Supplies furnished to pupils:
   a. What educational supplies shall be furnished pupils free?
   b. What educational supplies shall be sold pupils?
   c. Shall educational supplies which are sold to pupils be sold
      1) At cost?
      2) Below cost?
      3) At a profit?
2. Types and characteristics:
   a. What shall be the general type or characteristics of the educational supplies purchased?
3. Appropriations:
   a. What shall be the annual appropriation for educational supplies for the respective buildings and divisions of the schools?
4. Storage and distribution:
   a. What storage facilities and means of distribution shall be provided for handling educational supplies?
5. Purchase:
   a. What shall be the qualifications of the firms or persons from whom educational supplies are purchased?
6. Sale:
   a. Under what conditions shall educational supplies be sold?
7. Insurance:
   a. See Insurance of Buildings and Equipment, page 111.
8. Inventories:
   a. What inventories shall be made annually of educational supplies?

Administrative Jobs

These and like administrative jobs should be delegated to the superintendent of schools:

1. Advise the board of education as to the desirable types and characteristics of educational supplies to be purchased.
2. Ascertain the annual appropriation needed for educational supplies.
3. Select educational supplies.

4. Purchase educational supplies.
5. Store educational supplies.
6. Distribute educational supplies.
7. Pay for educational supplies.
8. Sell educational supplies.
9. Insure educational supplies (see Insurance of Buildings and Equipment, page 111).
10. Keep adequate records of all matters pertaining to educational supplies and submit appropriate reports thereof to the board of education.

PROBLEM OR JOB: NON-EDUCATIONAL SUPPLIES

See Educational Supplies, page 131.

PROBLEM OR JOB: TEXTBOOKS

Decisions made by a board of education on these and like issues are its policies:

1. Annual appropriation:
   a. What shall be the annual appropriation for textbooks?
      1) For first adoptions?
         a) For basic texts?
         b) For supplementary texts?
      2) For replacement purposes?
         a) For basic texts?
         b) For supplementary texts?
   b. What shall be the marginal appropriation to meet advances in prices of textbooks and emergency needs?
2. Free textbooks:
   a. Shall free textbooks be provided in the respective divisions of the school system?
   b. If free textbooks are not provided pupils,
      1) Shall the district handle the textbooks to be sold to the pupils?
      2) Shall the district provide teachers with copies of textbooks?
3. Textbooks of which the author is in the employ of the district:

a. May a textbook of which the author, co-author, or editor is in the employ of the district be used, if the author, co-author, or editor turns over to the district his income from the royalty resulting from the sale of his book to the district?

4. Selection:
    a. What viewpoints and attitudes on the following may textbooks selected for the public schools set forth?
        1) Patriotism?
        2) Evolution?

5. Worn and obsolete textbooks:
    a. How shall worn and obsolete textbooks be disposed of?

Administrative Jobs

These and like administrative jobs should be delegated to the superintendent of schools:

1. Select textbooks.
2. Purchase textbooks.
3. Replace textbooks.
4. Pay for textbooks.
5. Distribute textbooks.
6. Sell textbooks to pupils.
7. Collect author's royalty in case he is in employ of district.
8. Dispose of worn and obsolete textbooks.
9. Keep adequate records of textbooks and make appropriate reports to the board of education.

PROBLEM OR JOB: SCHOOL ELECTIONS

Decisions made by a board of education on these and like issues are its policies:

1. Purposes:
    a. For what purposes shall school elections be held?
2. Dates:
    a. What shall be the dates of the different elections?

Administrative Jobs

This and like administrative jobs should be delegated to the superintendent of schools:

1. Make arrangements for each of the elections to be held.

PROBLEM OR JOB: SCHOOL LEGISLATION

Decisions made by a board of education on these and like issues are its policies:

1. How influence:
   a. What efforts shall the school district make to secure desired school legislation?
2. Appropriations:
   a. What annual appropriation shall be made to cover expenses incurred in seeking to secure desired legislation?

Administrative Jobs

These and like administrative jobs should be delegated to the superintendent of schools:

1. Have such efforts made to secure desired legislation as the policies of the board require.
2. Ascertain the annual appropriation needed to pay expenses incurred in seeking legislation.
3. Pay such expenses.
4. Keep adequate records of all matters pertaining to school legislation and submit appropriate reports thereof to the board of education.

PROBLEM OR JOB: LEGAL SERVICE

Decisions made by a board of education on these and like issues are its policies:

1. Appropriations:
   a. What shall be the annual appropriation for legal services?
2. Selection of attorneys.
   a. What shall be the bases for the selection of attorneys?
   b. Shall the attorneys nominated by the superintendent of schools be approved?
3. Organization:
   a. If a legal department is maintained, what shall be its organization and relation to the other departments of the school system?

Administrative Jobs

These and like administrative jobs should be delegated to the superintendent of schools:

1. Ascertain the annual appropriation needed for legal services.
2. Select attorneys and submit their names to the board of education for approval.
3. Pay attorneys.
4. Keep adequate records of all matters pertaining to legal services and submit appropriate reports thereof to the board of education.

PROBLEM OR JOB: COURT ORDERS AND WRITS

Decisions made by a board of education on this and like issues are its policies:
1. How handled:
   a. How shall each of the following court orders or writs be handled?
      1) Attachments of salaries and wages.
      2) Attested accounts.
      3) Escrows.
      4) Orders in aid of execution.
      5) Mechanics' liens.

Administrative Jobs

These and like administrative jobs should be delegated to the superintendent of schools:
1. Carry out the policies of the board with respect to court orders and writs.
2. Keep adequate records of court orders and writs and submit adequate reports thereof to the board of education.

PROBLEM OR JOB: DEPOSITORIES

Decisions made by a board of education on these and like issues are its policies:
1. Qualifications:
   a. What shall be the qualifications of depositories?
2. Selection:
   a. What shall be the procedure to be used in the selection of depositories?
   b. Shall the depositories selected by the superintendent of schools be approved?

3. Bond:
   a. What shall be the bond required of depositories?
4. Deposits:
   a. What funds shall be placed in the respective depositories?
   b. What shall be the maximum deposit in each depository?
5. Withdrawals:
   a. What policy shall govern withdrawals from the respective depositories?
6. Overdrafts:
   a. On what conditions may overdrafts be made on the respective depositories?
   b. How large may be the overdrafts on each depository?
   c. How shall overdrafts be handled?

Administrative Jobs

These and like administrative jobs should be delegated to the superintendent of schools:

1. Select depositories and submit these to the board of education for its approval.
2. Accept or reject the bond of the respective depositories in accordance with the policies of the board.
3. Place such funds in the respective depositories as the policies of the board require.
4. Make withdrawals from depositories.
5. Administer overdrafts on depositories in accordance with the policies of the board.
6. Keep adequate records of all matters pertaining to depositories and submit appropriate reports thereof to the board of education.

PROBLEM OR JOB: INVESTMENTS

Decisions made by a board of education on these and like issues are its policies:

1. Of what funds:
   a. What funds shall be invested?
2. In what:
   a. Shall investments be made in
      1) Bonds?
      2) Building and loan stock?

3) Real estate?
b. By what criteria shall the bonds, stocks, etc., be selected for investment?
c. Shall the investments by the superintendent of schools be approved?
3. Interest:
a. Into what funds shall the income from investments be placed?

Administrative Jobs

These and like administrative jobs should be delegated to the superintendent of schools:
1. Advise the board of education relative to the funds available for investment.
2. Make such investments as authorized by the board.
3. Collect interest on investments and place this in the funds designated by the board of education.
4. Keep adequate records of all matters pertaining to investments and submit appropriate reports thereof to the board of education.

Problem or Job: THE FISCAL YEAR

Decisions made by a board of education on these and like issues are its policies:
1. Adoption:
a. What shall be the fiscal year?
2. Change:
a. Under what conditions shall the fiscal year be changed?
b. Shall the change in the fiscal year recommended by the superintendent of schools be made?

Administrative Jobs

This and like administrative jobs should be delegated to the superintendent of schools:
1. Advise the board of education as to desirable changes in the fiscal year.

PROBLEM OR JOB: THE BUDGET

Decisions made by a board of education on these and like issues are its policies:

1. Preparation and adoption:
    a. When shall the budget be prepared and adopted?
    b. Shall the budget prepared by the superintendent of schools be adopted?
2. Form and content:
    a. What shall be the form and content of the budget?
3. Transfer of funds:
    a. What policy shall govern the transfer of funds in the budget?

Administrative Jobs

These and like administrative jobs should be delegated to the superintendent of schools:

1. Prepare the budget and submit it to the board of education for approval.
2. Administer the budget in accordance with the policies of the board.
3. Keep adequate records of all matters pertaining to the budget and submit appropriate reports thereof to the board of education.

PROBLEM OR JOB: TAXES

Decisions made by a board of education on these and like issues are its policies:

1. Levies:
    a. What shall be the levies for the respective funds?
2. Refunds:
    a. What policy shall govern the refund of taxes?
3. Collector:
    (In states where the district collects the tax)
    a. Qualifications:
        1) What shall be the qualifications of the tax collector?
    b. Salary:
        1) What shall be the remuneration of the tax collector?

   c. Selection and employment:
     1) Shall the person selected for tax collector by the superintendent of schools be approved?
   d. Bond:
     1) What shall be the bond of the tax collector?

Administrative Jobs

These and like administrative jobs should be delegated to the superintendent of schools:

1. Ascertain the levies necessary for the respective funds.
2. Make such refunds of taxes as the policies of the board require.
3. Nominate a person for tax collector and submit his name to the board for its approval.
4. Accept or reject the bond of the tax collector.
5. Place all tax receipts in the proper funds.
6. Keep adequate records of all matters pertaining to taxes and submit appropriate reports thereof to the board of education.

PROBLEM OR JOB: GIFTS TO SCHOOLS

Decisions made by a board of education on these and like issues are its policies:

1. Shall gifts to schools be accepted from citizens?
2. Shall pupils, school organizations, and graduating classes be encouraged to make gifts to the schools?
3. Which of the following types of gifts may be accepted?
   a. Economic
     Land
     Buildings
     Stadium
     Money
     Equipment
     Supplies
     Scholarships
     Services, such as auctioneering sites and buildings, etc.
   b. Art
     Paintings
     Sculpture

       Ceramics

       Photographs

  c. Religious

       Bibles

       Books

       Magazines

       Newspapers

  d. Patriotic

       Flags

       Memorials

  e. Museum specimens

4. Shall gifts bearing advertising of dance halls, pool halls, bowling alleys, soft drink parlors, theaters, and the like be accepted?

5. Shall gifts carrying any religious allusions or advertising be accepted?

6. Shall gifts be accepted on the condition
   a. That the name of the donor be announced once or at intervals?
   b. That the name of the donor be printed on or attached to the gift?
   c. That the name, business, or other advertising of the donor be placed on the gift?

7. Shall the school district obligate itself as to the use of a gift?

8. Shall the school district obligate itself as to the placement of a gift?

9. What recognition of the acceptance of a gift shall the school district make?

Administrative Jobs

These and like administrative jobs should be delegated to the superintendent of schools:

1. Receive offers of gifts.
2. Accept offers of gifts.
3. Reject offers of gifts.
4. Accept the gift.
5. Acknowledge receipt of the gift.
6. Place the gift.
7. Formulate rules for the use of the gift.

8. Enforce rules for the use of the gift.
9. Report to the board of education the action taken on jobs 1–8.
10. Keep adequate records of gifts.

Problem or Job: SPECIAL ASSESSMENTS

Decisions made by a board of education on this and like issues are its policies:

1. Appropriation:
   a. What shall be the annual appropriation for the payment of special assessments levied against school district property?

Administrative Jobs

These and like administrative jobs should be delegated to the superintendent of schools:

1. Ascertain the annual appropriation needed to pay special assessments.
2. Pay special assessments.
3. Keep adequate records of all matters pertaining to special assessments and submit appropriate reports thereof to the board of education.

Problem or Job: EMPLOYEES' BONDS

Decisions made by a board of education on this and like issues are its policies:

1. Of whom required:
   a. What bonds shall be required of the respective school employees?

Administrative Jobs

These and like administrative jobs should be delegated to the superintendent of schools:

1. Advise the board of education as to the bonds that should be required of the respective employees.
2. Accept or reject bonds of employees in accordance with the policies of the board of education.
3. Keep adequate records of all matters pertaining to employees' bonds and make appropriate reports thereof to the board of education.

PROBLEM OR JOB: LOANS

Decisions made by a board of education on these and like issues are its policies:

1. Purposes:
   a. For which of the following purposes may the district borrow?
      1) Purchase of grounds.
      2) Improvement of grounds.
      3) Construction of buildings.
      4) Alteration and repair of buildings.
      5) Purchase of equipment.
      6) Purchase of supplies.
      7) Salaries and wages.
   b. Under what conditions may loans be made for each of the above purposes?
2. Forms:
   a. Which of the following forms shall be made use of it borrowing for each of the purposes that are listed in 1 above?
      1) Overdrafts.
         (See Overdrafts, under Depositories, page 136.)
      2) Notes.
         (See Notes, page 143.)
      3) Bonds.
         (See Bonds, page 143.)
         a) Straight bonds.
         b) Sinking fund bonds.
         c) Serial bonds.

Administrative Jobs

These and like administrative jobs should be delegated to the superintendent of schools:

1. Advise the board of education as to need for and the desirability of making loans.
2. Make recommendations to the board as to the kind of loans that should be made.
3. Negotiate the loans authorized by the school board.
4. See Overdrafts, page 136; Notes, page 143; and Bonds, page 143.

PROBLEM OR JOB: NOTES

Decisions made by a board of education on these and like issues are its policies:

1. Purposes:

    a. For what purposes and under what conditions shall notes be used in borrowing money?

2. Form and content:

    a. What shall be the form and content of notes issued?

3. Size:

    a. In what sums shall notes for each loan be issued?

4. Interest:

    a. What shall be the rate of interest on notes for each loan?

5. Term:

    a. What shall be the term of the respective notes in each loan?

6. Sale:

    a. By what procedure shall notes be sold?

7. Payment:

    a. What arrangement shall be made for making payments on notes and the interest thereon?

Administrative Jobs

These and like administrative jobs should be delegated to the superintendent of schools:

1. Advise the board of education relative to all matters pertaining to the issuance and payment of notes.

2. Negotiate the sale of notes.

3. Pay notes and the interest thereon.

4. Keep adequate records of all matters pertaining to the notes and submit appropriate reports thereon to the board.

PROBLEM OR JOB: BONDS

(See Loans, page 142).

Decisions made by a board of education on these and like issues are its policies:

1. Purpose:

    a. For what purposes and in what amounts shall bonds be issued?

2. Kind:
   a. Which of the following kinds of bonds shall be issued:
      1) Straight bonds?
      2) Sinking fund bonds?
      3) Serial bonds?
3. Denominations:
   a. In what denominations shall bonds be issued?
4. Term:
   a. For what terms shall bonds be issued?
5. Interest:
   a. What shall be the rates of interest on bonds?
6. Election:
   a. On what date shall the bond election be held?
   b. What arrangements shall be made in preparation for the bond election?
7. Sale:
   a. On what date shall bonds be sold?
   b. What arrangements shall be made for the sale of bonds?
8. Payment:
   a. What arrangements shall be made for the payment of bonds and interest thereon?

Administrative Jobs

These and like administrative jobs should be delegated to the superintendent of schools:

1. Advise the board of education on all matters pertaining to school bonds.
2. Make arrangements for bond elections and for the sale and retirement of bonds.
3. Sell bonds.
4. Pay interest on bonds.
5. Pay bonds.
6. Keep adequate records on all matters pertaining to school bonds and submit appropriate reports thereof to the board of education.

PROBLEM OR JOB: FUNDS OF SCHOOL ORGANIZATIONS

Decisions made by a board of education on these and like issues are its policies:

1. How administered and by whom:
    a. How shall the funds of clubs, classes, and other organizations within the schools be administered?
    b. By whom shall such funds be administered?

Administrative Jobs

These and like administrative jobs should be delegated to the superintendent of schools:

1. Advise the board of education relative to the administering of funds of school organizations.
2. See that the funds of school organizations are administered as the policies of the board require.

PROBLEM OR JOB: DEFICITS

Decisions made by a board of education on these and like issues are its policies:

1. When made:
    a. Under what conditions may deficits be incurred in the respective funds?
2. How met:
    a. What arrangements shall be made to provide for meeting deficits?

Administrative Jobs

These and like administrative jobs should be delegated to the superintendent of schools:

1. Administer deficits in accordance with the policies of the board of education.
2. Keep adequate records of all matters pertaining to deficits and submit appropriate reports thereof to the board of education.

PROBLEM OR JOB: PAYROLLS

Decisions made by a board of education on this and like issues are its policies:

1. How administered:
    a. How shall the respective payrolls of the school be administered?

Administrative Jobs

These and like administrative jobs should be delegated to the superintendent of schools:

1. Administer the respective payrolls in accordance with the policies of the board.
2. Keep adequate records of all matters pertaining to payrolls and submit appropriate reports thereof to the board of education.

PROBLEM OR JOB: LOST WARRANTS AND CHECKS

Decisions made by a board of education on these and like issues are its policies:

1. Duplicates:
   a. Shall duplicates be issued for lost warrants and checks?
   b. Under what conditions shall such duplicates of warrants or checks be issued?

Administrative Jobs

These and like administrative jobs should be delegated to the superintendent of schools:

1. Issue duplicate warrants and checks in accordance with the policies of the board.
2. Keep adequate records of all matters pertaining to lost warrants and checks and submit appropriate reports thereof to the board of education.

PROBLEM OR JOB: ACCOUNTING SYSTEM

Decisions made by a board of education on these and like issues are its policies:

1. Adoption:
   a. What system of accounting shall be used by the school district?
2. Changes:
   a. What changes shall be made in the accounting system used?

Administrative Jobs

This and like administrative jobs should be delegated to the superintendent of schools:

1. Advise the board of education on the kind of accounting system that should be used and the changes that should be made in it from time to time.

PROBLEM OR JOB: AUDITS

Decisions made by a board of education on these and like issues are its policies:

1. To be made:
   a. What audits shall be made of monthly bills?
   b. What audits shall be made of the respective school offices handling school funds?

Note: When the problem of audits is subjected to the criteria set up in Chapter I, it is seen that auditing is an administrative detail. Being an administrative detail, an audit should not be made by a committee of the board. Instead, the board should employ a competent auditor, who is independent of the superintendent and responsible solely and directly to the board of · education.

PROBLEM OR JOB: FREIGHT AND DRAYAGE

Decisions made by a board of education on this and like issues are its policies:

1. Appropriations:
   a. What shall be the annual appropriations for freight and drayage?

Administrative Jobs

These and like administrative jobs should be delegated to the superintendent of schools:

1. Ascertain the annual appropriation needed for freight and drayage.
2. Pay freight and drayage charges.
3. Keep adequate records of all matters pertaining to freight and drayage and submit appropriate reports thereof to the board of education.

PROBLEM OR JOB: AUTOMOBILES AND BICYCLES

Decisions made by a board of education on these and like issues are its policies:

1. Space for parking and storage:
   a. What space shall be provided at the respective schools for the parking and storage of automobiles and bicycles?
2. Rules governing:
   a. What rules shall govern the use of bicycles and automobiles on school premises?

Administrative Jobs

These and like administrative jobs should be delegated to the superintendent of schools:

1. Advise the board of education as to
   a. Parking and storage space needed at each school.
   b. Rules that should govern the operation of automobiles and bicycles on school premises.
2. Enforce the policies of the board relating to the operation of automobiles and bicycles on school premises.

PROBLEM OR JOB: MISCELLANEOUS EMPLOYEES

Decisions made by a board of education on this and like issues are its policies:

1. Appropriations:
   a. What shall be the annual appropriation for miscellaneous employees?

Administrative Jobs

These and like administrative jobs should be delegated to the superintendent of schools:

1. Ascertain the annual appropriation needed for miscellaneous employees.
2. Hire miscellaneous employees.
3. Pay such employees.
4. Keep adequate records of all matters pertaining to miscellaneous employees and submit appropriate reports thereof to the board of education.

PROBLEM OR JOB: SALE OF SALVAGE AND DISCARDED
EQUIPMENT

Decisions made by a board of education on these and like
issues are its policies:
1. How conducted:
   a. How shall sales of salvage and discarded equipment be
   conducted?
2. Income:
   a. Into what funds shall the income from such sales be
   placed?

Administrative Jobs

These and like administrative jobs should be delegated to the
superintendent of schools:
1. Sell salvage and discarded equipment as required by the
   policies of the board.
2. Place the income from such sales in the funds designated
   by the board of education.
3. Keep adequate records of all matters pertaining to the sale
   of salvage and discarded equipment and submit an appropriate report thereof to the board of education.

———

PROBLEM OR JOB: DISPOSAL OF TRASH AND GARBAGE

Decisions made by a board of education on these and like
issues are its policies:
1. Method:
   a. How shall trash and garbage be disposed of?
2. Appropriation:
   a. What shall be the annual appropriation for the disposal
   of trash and garbage?

Administrative Jobs

These and like administrative jobs should be delegated to the
superintendent of schools:
1. Dispose of trash and garbage as the policies of the board
   require.
2. Ascertain the annual appropriation for this purpose.
3. Keep adequate records of all matters pertaining to the

disposal of trash and garbage and submit appropriate reports thereof to the board of education.

***

Problem or Job: LAUNDRY WORK

Decisions made by a board of education on this and like issues are its policies:

1. Appropriation:
   a. What shall be the annual appropriation for laundry work?

Administrative Jobs

These and like administrative jobs should be delegated to the superintendent of schools:

1. Ascertain the annual appropriation needed for laundry work.
2. Have laundry work done.
3. Pay for laundry work.
4. Keep adequate records of all matters pertaining to laundry work and submit appropriate reports thereof to the board of education.

***

Problem or Job: SCHOOL TIME

Decisions made by a board of education on this and like issues are its policies:

1. Standard or daylight-saving:
   a. Shall the schools be conducted on standard or daylight-saving time?

Administrative Jobs

This and like administrative jobs should be delegated to the superintendent of schools:

1. Conduct the schools on the time required by the board policies.

***

Problem or Job: NO-SCHOOL SIGNALS

Decisions made by a board of education on this and like issues are its policies:

1. Provisions:

a. What provisions shall be made for No-School Signals?

b. What sum may the superintendent expend annually for No-School Signals?

Administrative Jobs

This and like administrative jobs should be delegated to the superintendent of schools:

1. Make arrangements for such No-School Signals as the policies of the board require.

PROBLEM OR JOB: STATE DEPARTMENT OF EDUCATION

Decisions made by a board of education on these and like issues are its policies:

1. State aid:
   a. Which of the following forms of aid shall be sought or accepted from the State Department of Education?
      1) Financial
         a.) State apportionment
         b.) Aid for training teachers
         c.) Aid for vocational work
      2) Inspectional and advisory
         a) Courses of study
         b) Instruction
         c) Buildings and grounds
         d) Architect's plans
         e) Equipment
         f) Supplies
         g) Interpretation of law

Administrative Jobs

These and like administrative jobs should be delegated to the superintendent of schools:

1. Advise the board of education on the aid that should be sought and accepted from the State Department of Education.
2. Make arrangements with the State Department for the execution of the board's policies on these matters.
3. Make the required reports to the State Department of Education.

4. Keep adequate records of all matters pertaining to the State Department of Education and submit appropriate reports thereof to the board of education.

———

Problem or Job: SCHOOL SURVEYS

Decisions made by a board of education on these and like issues are its policies:
1. To be made:
   a. What school surveys shall be made?
2. Appropriations:
   a. What shall be the appropriation for such surveys?
3. By whom made:
   a. Shall the nominations of the superintendent for making surveys be approved?
4. Adoption of the survey report:
   a. Shall the survey report be approved and the recommendations adopted?

Administrative Jobs

These and like administrative jobs should be delegated to the superintendent of schools:
1. Advise the board on the desirability of having surveys made and on what should be included in such surveys.
2. Ascertain the appropriation needed for making such surveys.
3. Make arrangements for the making of such surveys as the board authorizes.
4. Pay survey staff.
5. Keep adequate records of all matters pertaining to the school surveys and submit appropriate reports thereof to the board of education.

———

Problem or Job: EDUCATIONAL, CIVIC, SOCIAL, RE-LIGIOUS, AND BUSINESS ORGANIZATIONS OF THE CITY

Decisions made by a board of education on this and like issues are its policies:
1. Coöperation:
   a. In promoting the educational program, how shall the district coöperate with

1) The City Council?
2) Chambers of Commerce?
3) The Rotary Club?
4) The Kiwanis Club?
5) The Lions Club?
6) The churches?
7) Parent-Teacher Associations?
8) Women's clubs?
9) Improvement clubs?
10) Non-public schools?
11) Colleges and universities?

Administrative Jobs

These and like administrative jobs should be delegated to the superintendent of schools:

1. Advise the board of education as to desirable methods of coöperating with these organizations.
2. Coöperate with these organizations as the policies of the board require.
3. Keep adequate records of coöperation with these organizations and submit appropriate reports thereof to the board of education.

PROBLEM OR JOB: SCHOOL REPORTS AND PUBLICITY

Decisions made by a board of education on these and like issues are its policies:

1. Kind:
   a. What kind of reports and publicity shall be made of the work of the public schools?
2. Appropriation:
   a. What shall be the annual appropriation for school reports and publicity?

Administrative Jobs

These and like administrative jobs should be delegated to the superintendent of schools:

1. Advise the board of education as to desirable reports and publicity of school work.

2. Ascertain the annual appropriation needed for school reports and publicity.
3. Prepare reports and arrange for publicity work.
4. Keep adequate records of all matters pertaining to school reports and publicity and submit appropriate reports thereof to the board of education.

CHAPTER III

HOW A BOARD OF EDUCATION SHOULD DO ITS WORK

Summary of Preceding Chapters

In Chapter I an analysis was made of previous studies on the work of boards of education. It was shown that the next important step in school administration is a determination of the part a board of education should assume in handling the administrative problems and jobs occurring in conducting a public school system. Criteria were established by means of which the respective duties and responsibilities of a board of education and of its chief executive officer could be determined and assigned.

Chapter II presents an analysis of the problems and jobs found to have occurred in administering more than a dozen public school systems. For each of these problems and jobs the functions of the board of education and of the superintendent of schools, respectively, were set forth in the light of criteria developed in Chapter I. It was admitted that a board of education has the legal right and authority to do any and all of the work in administering its school system, but it was contended that for a board to attempt to do more than that assigned it in Chapter II leads to inefficient administration and divided responsibility.

It has been pointed out that the board of education is recognized as the body responsible to the people of the district for the educational program of the school district. The work of the school district has been analyzed and assigned so as to leave full control of the school system in the board of education. The technical, professional, and administrative functions have been delegated to the employed professional chief executive.

Purpose of Chapter III

It is the purpose of this chapter to discover how a board of education should do its work in order that it may exercise the proper control over its schools and that the school system may be most efficiently administered.

Control Rests in Board as a Unit

In considering how a board of education should function, it must be borne in mind that authority and responsibility are located in the board acting as a unit. Dr. Cubberley in the following paragraphs makes this very clear.

Boards for school control in our cities to-day, as the successors of the town or district meeting, now represent the people in the matter of schools, and through such boards the people now exercise control over the education provided at public expense for their children. The school board members are merely citizens, selected as their representatives by the people of the community. As individuals they are still citizens: only when the board is in formal session do they have any actual authority.

It is the board, acting as a body, which in the name of the people controls the schools, and not the individual members who, when in session, compose it. Even when the board is in formal session, the individual members have only a voice and a vote, and their control over the schools is through the votes whereby rules, regulations, and policies are adopted. To have authority otherwise the authority must be expressly delegated to a member by the board as a body, and by a vote, and his authority then extends only so far as specified by such vote of the board. Members, to be sure, often attempt to exercise authority at other times, and frequently do so, but such authority is usurped authority and authority for which there is little or no legal right.[1]

Authority being placed in the board as a unit, the problem confronting it is how to exercise that authority so as to provide a system of administration in which responsibility can be definitely fixed and in which control remains for the board as a whole. The scheme of administration must require a minimum of time and energy on the part of board members and it must be such that the schools are administered efficiently. Delay and waste must be reduced to the minimum and results must be the best that can be produced for the money expended. Moreover, as has been developed in the previous chapters, the scheme of administration must be such as to make the best use of the employed professional talent.

Standing Committees

For some time evidence has been accumulating to show that committees have a tendency to determine policies and to control the schools by virtue of the fact that the board usually accepts and adopts committee reports and recommendations without adequate consideration and without change.

[1] Cubberley, E. P. *Public School Administration.* Houghton Mifflin Company, pp. 109–10, 1916.

The Springfield School Survey showed that during the five-year period, 1918–1922, the Springfield School Committee accepted and adopted without change 214 of the 217 committee reports presented during that period. Commenting on this, the Survey Commission says:

The illustrations given above show that the Springfield School Committee acts very largely through standing and special committees and that these committees are more likely to determine school policies than is the School Committee as a whole.[2]

Goodnow and Howe report as follows of committee functioning in the work of the New York City Board of Education:

A page by page examination of the minutes for six consecutive meetings in 1911, for example, disclosed that there were reported by committees at those meetings a total of 348 resolutions. Of these all but five were adopted unanimously at the meeting at which they were introduced *without discussion*.

A similar examination of the minutes for five consecutive meetings, late in 1912, yields an equally decisive result, 192 out of 194 resolutions on administrative matters reported by committee having been adopted by unanimous vote and without discussion upon their first presentation. The evidence of these two sets of figures, chosen at random, could be duplicated by similar figures obtained from any part of the minutes.[3]

In another place in the same report is found the following:

The action of the board upon such matters is, and must be, as above demonstrated, wholly perfunctory, a mere *pro forma* ratification of the action of the committee under whose jurisdiction the matter comes. A perfectly natural and predictable result of this practice is the development on the part of members and committees of a feeling of diplomatic courtesy, which militates against real consideration by the board of committee recommendations; a feeling that each committee is, within its own sphere, to all intents and purposes the board itself; and a consequent resentment on the part of committee members toward any attempt by a member of the board not on the committee to question its action or recommendation on the floor.

The degree to which this attitude is cherished by some of the members of the board was strikingly revealed at the meeting of the board held January 8, 1913. The Committee on Sites, having presented for adoption a resolution for the purchase of a particular site, a member requested that the committee present to the Board statistical information bearing on the necessity for such purchase. Upon the committee member having the matter in charge

---

[2] *Report of the Survey of Certain Aspects of the Public School System of Springfield, Massachusetts, 1923–1924*, Division of Field Studies, Teachers College, Columbia University, p. 29.

[3] Goodnow, F. J., and Howe, F. C. *The Organization, Status and Procedure of the Department of Education, City of New York, 1911–1913*, p. 144.

confessing his inability to supply such information at that time, the interested
member requested that the matter be laid over until the following meeting,
when such information might be forthcoming. This request seemed so un-
reasonable to another member of the Committee on Sites, and so at variance
with the prerogatives of a member, that he moved that this member be
appointed a committee of one to investigate and report to the board the
existence of any facts tending to justify his lack of confidence in the committee.

In the presence of such a spirit as this, a private member will hardly feel
inclined to question the report of a committee merely because he is not convinced by the facts, or lack of facts, presented by the committee. Most
members, certainly all those not of an aggressive turn, will accept without
question the report of the committee, unless they have very good reason for
not doing so.[4]

Goodnow and Howe summarize their recommendations on
standing committees as follows:

That the present committee organization be abolished, and that in its place
there be organized only such committees as are found by experience to be
desirable for the purpose of preparing, for the real consideration of the Board,
information upon matters of fundamental, legislative, and inspectorial character, leaving to the paid officers and employees of the Board all purely
administrative and technical matters; and that, during the continuance of
the present provisions of the Charter, imposing upon the Board or its Executive
Committee the performance of administrative duties, the Executive Committee
to be reëmpowered to discharge those duties; with a view, however, to the
eventual repeal of the charter provisions in question.[5]

The Atlanta School Survey recommended the abolishment of
standing committees as follows:

The Board of Education may very adequately render the service necessary
in the control and regulation of the school system of Atlanta by eliminating
its standing committees. Whenever committee action is desired, special
committees may be appointed which should perform the service required and
then should cease to exist.

It is recommended that the Board develop a new organization which will
tend toward the elimination of the standing committees and which will
recognize the superintendent of schools and his administrative staff as the
proper agencies for the performance of all executive acts, the Board reserving
to itself the legislative powers essential in the development and control of a
large organization.[6]

The Providence School Survey makes the following recommendation with respect to standing committees:

[4] Goodnow, F. J. and Howe, F. C. *op. cit.*, pp. 150–51.
[5] *Ibid.*, pp. 195–96.
[6] *Report of the Survey of the Public School System of Atlanta, Ga., 1922*, Division of Field Studies,
Teachers College, Columbia University, pp. 14–15.

That the School Committee act as a committee of the whole in considering and passing upon the program and particular recommendations of the superintendent of schools, and that all standing committees be abolished.[7]

The following are the recommendations of the Watertown School Survey with respect to standing committees:

Careful study of the work done by the standing committees of the Watertown Board of Education as it is recorded in the minutes of the board from which the preceding extracts were selected, leads to the following conclusions:

a) That on the whole the standing committees perform routine functions that ought to be performed by professional executives employed by the board. A study of the efforts of the finance committee to audit the bills and payrolls is a case in point, as is also the unorganized method of purchasing.

b) That when members of a board of education take upon themselves routine tasks such as those performed by the members of the Watertown board, the burdens of school board members become such that many competent citizens hesitate to permit themselves to be appointed or elected to the school board.

c) That at times these committees are delegated to pass upon matters that are purely professional in their scope—matters that should be left to the professional executives employed.

d) That because of the amount of work the Watertown Board of Education attempts to pass upon, it not infrequently happens that committee policies become board policies without receiving the careful consideration of the board as a whole. That such is the case is made evident by the fact that committee recommendations and reports are almost invariably adopted as submitted by a unanimous vote of the board.

e) That such an organization of standing committees performing so wide a range of duties, many of which are purely executive in character, prevents that board from functioning effectively as a policy-formulating body which looks ahead and takes into consideration future needs as well as those of the present. The evidence seems to indicate that the Watertown board is so nearly overwhelmed with the details of the present that it does not have the opportunity to anticipate adequately the needs of the future.

The recommendation made by the survey committee involves the elimination of all such committees, the board itself meeting as a committee of the whole to discuss matters that need informal discussion before the formulation of a policy. In this way every member of the board would be thoroughly familiar with every policy before it is finally approved. From time to time, as need arises, special committees may be appointed which will perform specific tasks assigned them by the board and then cease to exist when that specific duty has been performed. If purely routine and executive matters are delegated to the professional executives employed by the board, then the board will have time to discuss in detail the policies to be formulated, and

[7] *Report of the Survey of Certain Aspects of the Public School System, Providence, Rhode Island, 1923-24*, Division of Field Studies, Teachers College, Columbia University, p. 25.

give attention to the planning of a comprehensive program for the future as well as for the present.[8]

The following extracts from other educational literature emphasize the desirability of abolishing standing committees:

All board legislation should be based upon the deliberations of the entire board, rather than being referred to standing committees. [9]

It is important that a board of education consider the program and policies proposed by the superintendent of schools as a board and not in separate committees which report to the general body. There may be times when a special committee of the board may prove useful in reviewing carefully with the executive officer or his associates some problems requiring careful study from a layman's point of view. In such cases special committees should be appointed and their reports should be considered along with the recommendation of the superintendent. Standing committees seem to me to be worse than useless. The chairman of a standing committee quite commonly comes to believe that he has some peculiar fitness or ability in the field represented by his committee and infrequently he will tend to assume the functions of the executive. When standing committees make reports which are accepted by boards of education, as a matter of senatorial courtesy one gets little careful consideration of the major issues to be passed upon by the board. [10]

The superintendent should be responsible to the board as a whole, and not to sub-committees or individual members. [11]

One of the first problems to which the Madison (Wisconsin) board of education devoted its attention in its plan of reorganization was the committee system which had been in operation for a considerable time. . . . After full discussion, the view prevailed that the committee system in general is not conducive to the efficient conduct of business. When the work of the board is done by committees, there is usually but little discussion by the entire board. Some of the members may be almost entirely ignorant of what the others are doing. A committee report is likely to be adopted although other members of the board have not given the question under consideration very serious attention. Thus, in effect important policies may be determined by a minority of the membership. In so far as recommendations from superintendents and other officials are concerned, it is just as easy to have these recommendations presented to the entire board for approval or rejection as it is to present them to a committee of three or four. In a similar way, plans for new construction should be studied and passed upon by the entire membership of the board instead of having the approval granted upon the recommendation of a small committee. [12]

[8] *Report of the Survey of the Schools of Watertown, N. Y., 1924–25*, Division of Field Studies, Teachers College, Columbia University, pp. 13–14.

[9] Jesse B. Sears. *The School Survey.* Houghton Mifflin Company, p. 55, 1925.

[10] George D. Strayer. The Relation of Administrative Officers to Boards of Education. (In Department of Superintendence *First Yearbook*, 162, 1923.)

[11] Edwin C. Broome, "Strengthening the Superintendency." *Addresses and Proceedings of the N. E. A.*, 58: 508, 1920.

[12] Thos. W. Gosling (Superintendent of Schools, Madison, Wisconsin). "School Board Organization in a City of Forty Thousand." *American School Board Journal*, 69: 39, August, 1924.

Thus, quotation after quotation from authorities and from administrators in the field can be given to illustrate existing opinion concerning standing committees. Moreover, a movement has already started for the abolishment of standing committees. Among the cities which recently abolished standing committees are Des Moines, Iowa; Madison, Wisconsin; Montclair, New Jersey; and Springfield, Massachusetts. The Madison, Wisconsin, by-laws providing for action by the board as a whole, read as follows:

> All business before the board shall be transacted before the entire board, or a duly constituted quorum thereof, except that a standing committee consisting of the president, treasurer and one member elected by the board, shall audit, monthly, all expenditures which shall be duly authorized by the board. No other special or standing committees shall be appointed or elected by the board.[13]

Summarizing the preceding, relative to standing committees, it may be said that the evidence at hand shows a pronounced tendency on the part of board committees to determine school policies and to control the schools. This tendency is shown to be due to the fact that committee reports and recommendations are most frequently accepted and adopted without change and without adequate consideration by the board as a whole. Such functioning of a board leads to divided responsibility and inefficient administration. Furthermore, it fails to make the most profitable use of the employed professional talent and it makes for unwarranted demands on the time and energy of board members.

The Board a Committee of the Whole

Except for special and unusual situations, the board should function, therefore, as a committee of the whole. It should require of its superintendent of schools adequate and complete information on every phase of the school system in order that it may have at hand the basis for making intelligent decisions. All decisions of the board should be made only after consideration by the whole board. When the board has determined its policy on the problem in hand, it should leave the execution of it to the employed professional chief executive. It should then require such reports from him that it may know its policy is carried out.

[13] *Loc. cit.* 69: 39, August 1924.

It is of the utmost importance that the board consider only major issues. Only by the consideration of large issues and the determination of policies on these can the board really know the true condition of the school system and legislate wisely for its present and future administration. The board that seeks to pass judgment on every minor issue and detail loses its sense of perspective. It is so hurried in its consideration of small and innumerable problems, that it invariably fails to see the larger and more important issues of which these minor problems are a part.

The board that passes on each separate expenditure for books, that considers each individual tuition case, that weighs the desirability of each separate request for the installation of a telephone, that debates the desirability of each purchase of coal, that discusses how the soil of each school garden should be prepared for seeding, that authorizes each purchase of postage stamps, that evaluates each proposed purchase of kindergarten supplies, that decides the merits of each request for leave of absence, that determines whether or not a given school piano shall be tuned, that passes on each and every request for the use of school buildings by non-school groups, that considers the installation of glass in each of the doors or broken windows, and sundry minor items of necessity sees only a mass of details.

The board that spends time on these innumerable and comparatively trifling details thereby crowds out consideration of the really important problems. Moreover, consideration of the big problems perforce makes for the adequate control of the countless minor ones, for the major problems have in them as their elements all the lesser problems.

Each purchase of books is a part of the big problems of textbooks and libraries as these are analyzed in Chapter II. The installation of telephones, tuition cases, purchase of coal and postage stamps, tuning the piano, and all the other minor problems mentioned above are likewise parts of big problems, each of which is analyzed in the preceding chapter. The board that will pass on the large issues, such as those raised under these big problems in Chapter II, and will hold the chief executive responsible for carrying out its policies will exercise real control.

Evidence that some boards of education practice this policy is found in the following extract from the minutes of the Passaic (New Jersey) Board of Education:

Board of Education

LADIES AND GENTLEMEN:

Your Education Committee recommends that orders be placed for text-books for the school year, 1924–25 as are approved by the Superintendent of Schools, provided the cost does not exceed the amount placed in the budget for this purpose.

> EDWIN FLOWER
> IDA P. SYLVESTER
> R. D. BENSON
> JAMES A. CROWLEY

Moved by Commissioner Sylvester and seconded by Commissioner Terhune that the recommendation of the committee be adopted.

Carried unanimously on roll call vote. 4/14/24.

By way of contrasting good board procedure as illustrated in the preceding case, the following from a set of minutes also studied by the author is given.

The superintendent of schools recommended the purchase of a 5″ x 8″ kodak costing $75 "to make a record of good and interesting work done in the schools." This recommendation was referred to a committee of one to report back to the board. At a later meeting of the board this committee of one reported as follows, and his report was adopted unanimously on a roll call vote:

> The committee of one appointed to investigate the recommendation of the superintendent for the purchase of a camera, has looked into the matter and finds that the camera is not required for an educational feature, but for the use of the superintendent's office. He desires it for taking pictures sometimes of certain school activities. Such a camera can be purchased for not more than $30 and your committee recommends its purchase.

It should be added that this occurred in a school system spending more than $680,000 each year.

The method of procedure in school administration here advocated requires for its operation a highly trained professional chief executive possessing business acumen, vision, and courage. An illustration of a superintendent who for some reason failed to meet these requirements is given in the following quotations from a set of minutes.

> The building committee recommended that the old science table in the high school be transferred and installed in the high school annex at a cost of approximately $350. The president referred this matter to the superintendent.

In the minutes of a later meeting this entry is found:

> Moved by —— and seconded by —— that the matter of connecting up the science table in the high school annex be referred to the Building Committee with power. Carried unanimously on roll call vote.

The purchase of coal furnishes another excellent illustration of proper school board procedure as well as of the work of the superintendent. The analysis of this problem in Chapter II, page 128, provides for the actual purchase of coal by the superintendent or his subordinate in charge of this kind of work. One superintendent interviewed informed the author that he makes all the arrangements for the purchase of coal and then takes with him the president of the board to close the deal "so that it is clear I do not get a rake-off on the purchase." A little thought on the matter discloses that such procedure is no guarantee that rake-offs are not forthcoming to the superintendent.

On the other hand, the adequate consideration by the board of the whole problem of fuel as this is analyzed in the preceding chapter will give it full control of the problem and definitely fix responsibility.

It has been suggested that where experts, say on coal, are members of the board, such matters should be delegated to the board member who is the expert instead of to the superintendent. This suggestion is in direct violation of good administrative procedure. All administrative details should be delegated to the superintendent and he should be held responsible for their proper administration. In administering these jobs he will seek expert advice whenever and wherever it is available either from board members or from persons not members of the board. But his is the responsibility to perform all administrative jobs. Moreover, unless this policy is strictly adhered to, board members are likely to assume the rôle of expert in many fields and have many administrative jobs delegated to them.

An incorrect interpretation of what constitutes a board policy should be pointed out. A certain superintendent of schools was authorized by his board to equip one of the primary rooms in the system with a different type of furniture in order that a new kind of instruction could be had in this room. After the equipment of the room had been changed as authorized, the superintendent took this case as a precedent and without further authorization from his board proceeded to re-equip all the primary rooms in the school system. It is clear that such action by the superintendent was not in accord with the policy of the board. The situation should have been handled in accordance with the analysis of the problem in Chapter II.

MEETINGS OF THE BOARD

As nearly as possible all sessions of the board should be conducted in an informal fashion. That this should be so is readily seen when it is understood that the work of a board is deliberative and not argumentative. Only through informal meetings is it possible for each member of the board to contribute freely to the consideration of the problems at hand.

Except in rare or special instances, nothing should be introduced for consideration in board meetings unless it first has been submitted to the superintendent and he has prepared for the board all the available facts concerning it and incorporated these in a report to the board. The reports and recommendations of the superintendent to be considered at a meeting, should be sent to members of the board in advance of the meetings. By this procedure members can come to meetings of the board prepared to discuss intelligently each item of business to be considered.

Only in cases of appeal from the decision of the superintendent, and then only after it is clear that the superintendent cannot bring the matter to a settlement, should the board listen to and pass on communications and complaints. For a board to grant hearings on any and all matters, soon forces the board away from its true function over to the performance of tasks which should be delegated to the superintendent.

Study of the minutes of many cities shows that corrections in minutes are seldom made where minutes are read in board meetings. That this should be so is easily understood when the perfunctory method of reading minutes in board meetings is recalled.

It is therefore recommended that the reading of the minutes be dispensed with in board meetings. Instead, the minutes should be prepared immediately after each meeting of the board and copies of them sent to each member. If any correction is to be made in them, that fact can be pointed out in the next board meeting. Unless such correction is made, the minutes should stand approved as sent to the members.

SUMMARY

Control of the schools rests in the board of education acting as a unit. Because of the tendency of committees to determine policies and to control the schools by virtue of the fact that their reports are seldom carefully reviewed by the board, standing committee organization of school boards is undesirable. All administrative details should be delegated to the superintendent of schools, and policies and reports should invariably be considered by the board as a whole.

CHAPTER IV

SUMMARY AND CONCLUSIONS

Previous studies on the work of boards of education show that it is threefold: (1) to select the superintendent of schools; (2) to determine the policies of the school system; (3) to see to it that these policies are carried out by the superintendent of schools and his associates.

This study in Chapter I sets up criteria by means of which the respective duties and responsibilities of a school board and of its chief executive officer may be determined and assigned.

In Chapter II these criteria are applied to the problems and jobs actually found to occur in administering the schools of thirteen cities. The use of these criteria makes possible the easy determination of the respective duties and responsibilities of the board of education and of its superintendent of schools.

The work of Chapter III shows that the control of the schools rests in the board of education acting as a unit. It presents evidence to show that all standing committees should be abolished, that all administrative details should be delegated to the superintendent of schools, and that policies and reports should be considered by the board as a whole. Throughout the study it is made clear that the superintendent is the professional adviser to the board.

BIBLIOGRAPHY

BOOKS

CHAMBERLAIN, ARTHUR H. *The Growth of Responsibility and Enlargement of Power of the City School Superintendent.* University of California Press, Berkeley, California, 1913.

CUBBERLEY, ELLWOOD P. *Public School Administration.* Houghton Mifflin Company, 1916.

DOUGLASS, BENNETT C. *The Status of the Superintendent.* N. E. A. Department of Superintendence *First Yearbook,* 1: 4–152, 1913.

GOODNOW, F. J. and HOWE, F. C. *The Organization, Status, and Procedure of the Department of Education, City of New York, 1912–1913.*

MORRISON, JOHN CAYCE. *The Legal Status of the City Superintendent of Schools.* Teachers College, Columbia University, 1922.

SEARS, JESSE B. *The School Survey.* Houghton Mifflin Company, 1925.

STRAYER, GEORGE D., ENGELHARDT, N. L., and others. *Report of the Survey of Certain Aspects of the Public School System of Springfield, Massachusetts, 1923–1924.* Division of Field Studies, Teachers College, Columbia University.

STRAYER, GEORGE D., ENGELHARDT, N. L., and others. *Report of the Survey of Certain Aspects of the Public School System of Providence, Rhode Island, 1923–1924.* Division of Field Studies, Teachers College, Columbia University.

STRAYER, GEORGE D., ENGELHARDT, N. L., and others. *Report of the Survey of the Public School System of Atlanta, Georgia.* Division of Field Studies, Teachers College, Columbia University, 1922.

STRAYER, GEORGE D., ENGELHARDT, N. L., and others. *Report of the Survey of the Schools of Watertown, New York.* Division of Field Studies, Teachers College, Columbia University, New York City, 1925.

THEISEN, WILLIAM W. *The City Superintendent and the Board of Education.* Teachers College, Columbia University, 1917.

MISCELLANEOUS

BROOME, EDWIN C. "Strengthening the Superintendency." *Addresses and Proceedings of the National Education Association,* 58:508, 1920.

CHADSEY, CHARLES E. The Report of the Committee on the Status of the Superintendent (in the Department of Superintendence *First Yearbook,* pp. 156 ff, 1923).

EARLE, JESSE. "What About School Boards and Superintendents?" *American School Board Journal,* 68: 42, July, 1924.

GOSLING, THOS. W.   "School Board Organization in a City of Forty Thousand." *American School Board Journal*, 69:39, August, 1924.

HUNTER, FRED M.   "Professional Leadership of Superintendent."   *American Educational Digest*, 44:292, March, 1925.

STRAYER, GEORGE D.   "The Relation of Administrative Officers to Boards of Education."   The Department of Superintendence *First Yearbook*, 1:160 ff, 1923.

STUDEBAKER, J. W.   "School Board Organization and the Superintendent." *American School Board Journal*, 68: 37 ff, April, 1924.

APPENDIX

CITIES WHOSE MINUTES WERE USED AS THE BASIS FOR THIS
STUDY

CITY	POPULATION, 1920
Bronxville, New York	5,000
Lawrence, Kansas	12,456
Montclair, New Jersey	28,810
Watertown, New York	31,285
New Brunswick, New Jersey	32,779
York, Pennsylvania	47,512
Passaic, New Jersey	63,841
Bayonne, New Jersey	76,754
Des Moines, Iowa	126,468
Springfield, Massachusetts	129,614
Omaha, Nebraska	191,601
Providence, Rhode Island	237,595
Cleveland, Ohio	796,841

DATE DUE

DEMCO 38-297